Robinson Township Library
Robinson, Illinois 62454

Y0-AJJ-591

305.23   42762
Hol
Holbrook, Sabra
Growing up in France.

Robinson Township Library
Robinson, Illinois 62454

© THE BAKER & TAYLOR CO

BOOKS BY SABRA HOLBROOK

*The French Founders of North America
and Their Heritage*

Lafayette: Man in the Middle

Growing Up in France

Growing Up
in France

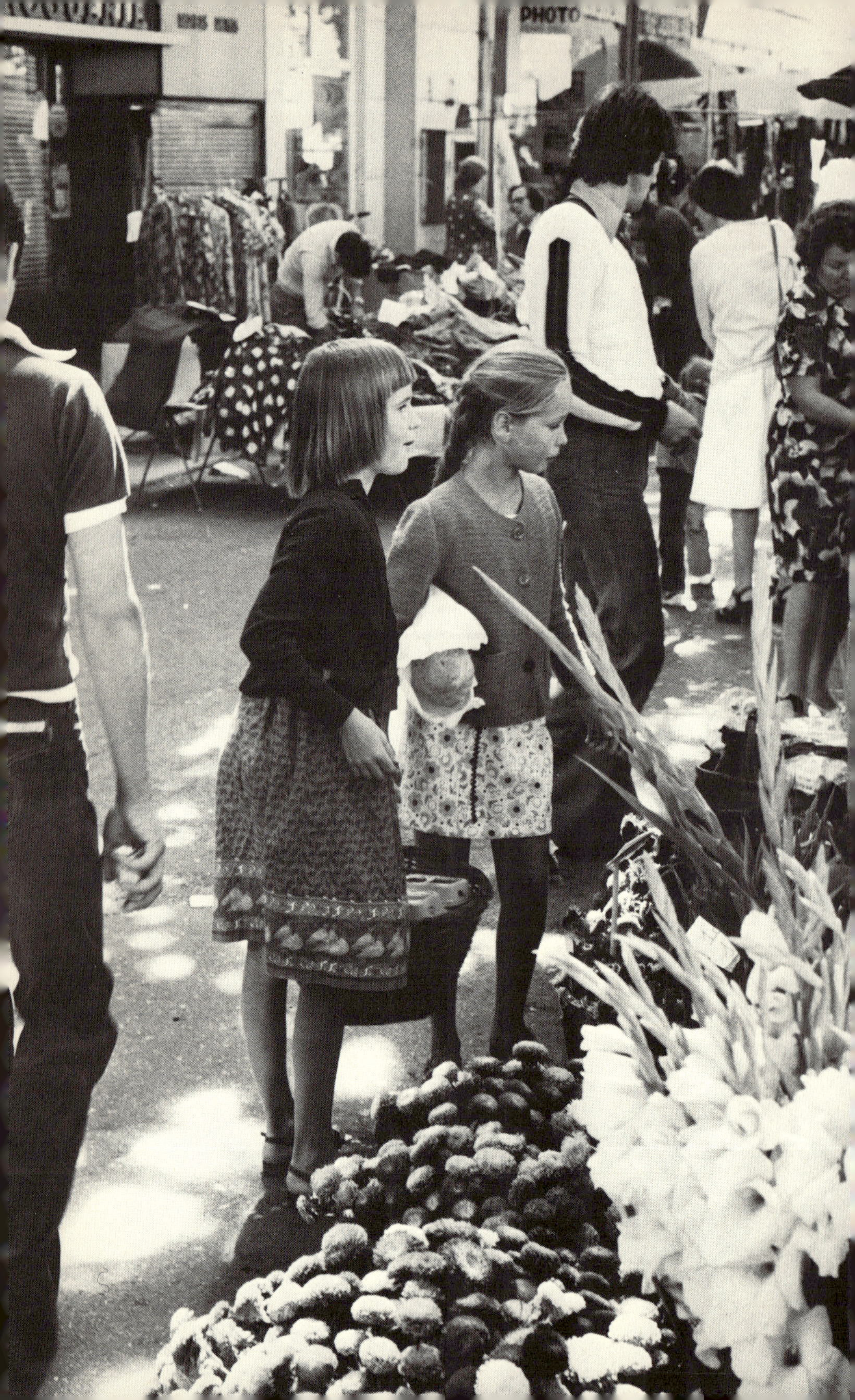
PHOTO

Sabra Holbrook

Growing Up in FRANCE

PHOTOGRAPHS BY NANCEE FENNESSEY
AND THOMAS WILE

1980

Atheneum · *New York*

LIBRARY OF CONGRESS CATALOGING IN PUBLICATION DATA

Holbrook, Sabra.   Growing up in France.

Bibliography: p. 101
Includes index.
SUMMARY: Text and photographs describe the daily activities
of children living in the cities and countryside of France.
1. Children—France—Juvenile literature.
[1. France—Social life and customs] I. Fennessey, Nancee.
II. Wile, Thomas.   III. Title.
HQ792.F7H6   301.43'14'0944   79-22101
ISBN 0-689-30745-4

Copyright © 1980 by Sabra Holbrook
All rights reserved
Published simultaneously in Canada by
McClelland & Stwart, Ltd.
Manufactured by The Halliday Lithograph Corporation
Hanover, Massachusetts
Designed by M. M. Ahern
First Edition

À Madeleine et Jean Ginestié,
avec ma reconnaissance de leur
efforts, vraiment formidables,
de m'aider dans la préparation
de ce livre. Et, il va sans
dire, avec toutes mes amitiés
affectueuses.

Contents

ACKNOWLEDGMENTS	xi
1. Weekend Fever	3
2. Families at Work	24
3. Welcome Back to School	32
4. Winter Specials	48
5. Returning Light	64
6. French With Spice	76
BIBLIOGRAPHY	101
FOR FURTHER READING	102
INDEX	104

A Word About This Book

ANTOINE, DOMINIQUE, ERIC, LAETITIA, and dozens of other children of France whom readers will meet in this book are flesh-and-blood children doing in the book what they do in their daily lives. The author has lived with French children in their homes, gone to school with them, camped with them, taken trips with them, picnicked with them, played their games, and celebrated their holidays. She has migrated to the mountains with *buron* families in Auvergne, fished with fathers and sons off the coast of Brittany, and linked arms with the singers of spontaneous Corsican songfests. This is her report on those experiences.

ACKNOWLEDGMENTS

I AM INDEBTED to many people over the many years I have traveled both the highways and byways of France for the background of this book. I mention here those who went out of their way—as, indeed, the French always do—to help me find what I sought during field research on the specific subject of children.

I acknowledge with warm gratitude their willingness to share with me whatever they knew that I needed to know. First, the children themselves. They are children of Alsatian, Jura, and Rhòne vineyard workers, especially Claude, Alain, René Stissel and their friends; children of the Beribiche, Aït-Khelifa, and Ketir families, especially Aziz, Dsamiila, Farida, and Yamina; Antoine Cecaldi; Antoine and Dominique de Champeaux; Bernard Brès; Bruno Gambini; Bruno Menaësse; Christine Attaccioli; and Didier brothers; Jégu and Philippe; Eric Belledent; Eric Tshatchérian; Fabienne Laurent; Fabienne Lucas; Florance Réhel; Frédérique Joumet; Frédéric Salvéry; Hervé Le Cozannet; Hocine Sennaorie; Jacques Colonna; Laetitia Guet; the Lcemétayer brothers, Dominique and Michel; Louis Besnard; the Macé children, David, Isabelle, and Valérie; grandchildren of Monsieur and Madame Édouard Bonnaud, especially Celline, Jean-Paul, Pascal, and Béatrice; Mireille

xii Acknowledgments

Paret; sons and daughters of the Moreno family, especially Émile, François, and Rose; Natherlie Niarfait; children of oystermen, especially Madeleine Courdavault and her friends; Pascale Ciabrini; Paul Giovanni; Philippe Olivier; Poetriciol Liobbé; the Rose children, Annabelle, Muriel, Pascal, and Patricia; the Rotterdam Troop of Boy and Girl Scouts in Strasbourg, especially Thomas Lavaux, Jean Paul Ledig, Rose and Mochel Pascal, and Claude Veltman; Sabine Jouval; Tour Armoise Cartel; Valérie Hochin; the Vecchio sisters, Valérie and Muriel; and Véronique Laude.

Next, the children's schools: Collège d'Education Secondaire near Colroy-La-Roche; Collège Marcel Pagnol, Pertuis; Collège d'Education Secondaire de Saint Lunéac; École de Chavaniac-Lafayette; École de la Grande Motte; École Primaire, Clermont-Ferrand; École Primaire, Colroy-La-Roche; École Publique de Glaine-Montaigut; École Publique de Lezoux; École Sainte Marie, Nant d'Aveyron; École Saint-Paul, Ajaccio, Corsica; L'École Sainte Thérèse, Montpellier; Institution Louis Martin, Montpellier; and Lycée Anna de Noailles, Evian.

And their teachers and school administrators: M. Adrien Decker, Mme. Andreani Annonciade, Mme. Balmes, M. Christian Bigay, Sister Elizabeth, M. Edouard Leryga, M. Jean Paul Simonet, Mme. Marie-Thérèse Robert, Mme. Monique Guarnieri, M. Robert Cariat, M. Jean-Claude Soulié, and M. Gil Soulié.

These government officials helped with information and introductions: M. Calvia, Delegué Régionale du Commissariat Général au Tourisme, Corsica; Mlle Nicole Garnier, Commissariat Général au Tourisme, Paris; M. Guillemoteau, Service d'Accueil de Pédagogues Étrangers; Mme. Simone Harari and her colleagues at the Secretariat d'État à la Jeunesse et aux Sports; Mr. George Hern, French Government Tourist Office, New York; and Mme.

Acknowledgments xiii

Monique Polgar, Service de Presse et d'Information, French Embassy, New York.

Parents, youth leaders and others close to children and contemporary affairs contributed viewpoints and opened access to situations strangers don't easily penetrate. Many times they offered priceless opportunities for learning in their own homes. These perceptive people were M. J. P. Aptel, leader of the Rotterdam Scout Troop in Strasbourg, and Mlle. Mireille Aptel; Mlle. Aït-Khelifa; Mme. Catherine Benedetti; M. Claude-Jean Bertrand; M. and Mme. Édourd Bonnaud; M. and Mme. de Champeaux; Mme. Le Cozanet; M. and Mme. J. F. Dassier; Mme. Adrien Decker; M. and Mme. Maurice Durand; M. and Mme. Marcel François and family; Dr. and Madame Jean Ginestié; M. and Mme. Gabriel Guet; M. Christophe Izard, Director, Children's Television, TFL; Mme. la Comptesse P. de Pontbriand; and Madame Catherine Wolik.

In addition I am grateful for the skilled technicians who worked around the clock with me, my photographers and long-suffering traveling companions, Nancee Fennessey and Tom Wile, and my typist, Lee Hennessy. I am also appreciative of the services of *Chez des Amis*, who arranged homestays for us with the Guet and de Champeaux families.

Growing Up in France

ENGLAND
N
BELGIUM
LUX.
GERMANY
English Channel
Le Havre
Paris
Strasbourg
Rhine River
Versailles
Seine River
VOSGES MTS.
BRITTANY
Pont L'Abbé
Pontivy
BURGUNDY
Loire River
Saône River
JURA MTS.
Autun
SWITZ.
Lake Geneva
FRANCE
Bay of Biscay
Evian
ALPS
Clermont-Ferrand
AUVERGNE
Lyon
Bordeaux
ITALY
Rhône River
Durance R.
Ardèche R.
MASSIF CENTRAL
Tarn River
Avignon
Apt
Pertuis
Bayonne
Biarritz
Montpellier
PROVENCE
Toulouse
Marseille
Mediterranean Sea
PYRENNEES
SPAIN
CORSICA
Ajaccio
Miles
0 50 100
0 100
Kms.
A. Karl/J. Kemp

I
Weekend Fever

LAETITIA GUET skips into her garden, swinging a basket of alfalfa and clover mixed with feathery carrot tops and a few thistles. Among clumps of cosmos, borders of petunias, and beds of zinnias and chrysanthemums, she has built a hutch for her black rabbit. Reaching it, she lifts a chickenwire flap and dumps the contents of her basket inside. Then she stands back, chewing gum, and watches her pet nibble.

The rabbit's name is Arthure. The e at the end of Arthur means the rabbit is female. Adding the e is like turning Louis into Louise.

Ten-year-old Laetitia lives on a farm in a part of southeast France called Provence. Her father's principal crop is carrots. He raises them organically—without the help of man-made chemicals. She and her parents and their friends dearly love the mountains that rib their region and the sheer gorges through which swift streams snake their way. "I am first of all Provençale and after that French," Laetitia claims in the musical accent of the south of France. That's what most Provençaux say.

They have good reason. Provence supplies the whole country with good things. Along a section of the southern shore, salt, mined from the Mediterranean Sea, stands in pyramids that gleam like snow. Sea salt is the only salt used by good French cooks. All grocery stores sell it. In the eighteenth century, taxes on this precious staple contributed to revolution.

In the marshy soil back from the coast are the paddies that provide all the rice French families can eat. Still farther inland olives grow in silvery groves, and peach and cherry orchards thrive. Beds of tender asparagus and rows of sweet, smooth-skinned melons nestle in valleys. Vineyards climb the hillsides, and on high plateaus mufflike clumps of lavender shoot up spikes of blossoms. The blossoms are harvested to make perfume. Sturdy cane and tall cyprus border the crops. They help shelter the crops from a mighty wind, the razor-sharp *mistral*.

Once Laetitia was caught on her bike when a mistral started. The wind blew her skirt right over her head. She hurried home, knowing that the gale's full force could easily turn her over. The mistral can even derail trains. It slashes unprotected crops and blasts down open chimneys. In spring and fall, Laetitia's father stuffs their chimney to keep the mistral out. But this fine autumn morning, no fear of it. The breeze is gentle, the sky clear. What a day to swim and canoe in the nearby Ardèche River!

Laetitia learned to swim in the Ardèche. Some of the cost of lessons was covered by local government and some by national government. Through an agency called the Secretariat of State for Youth and Sports, the national government spends what would amount to millions of dollars in American money on out-of-school activities for young people. Laetitia is one of seventeen million of them. They make up almost a third of the nation.

While watching Arthure, she begins to plan a trip to the Ardèche. Maybe her friend Véronique can come too. Not much more time for swimming before school starts again, mid-September. Suddenly her train of thought is interrupted. Scuffle, scuffle in the hedge surrounding the garden. Arthure has escaped from the hutch!

Weekend Fever

Laetitia had forgotten to latch the chickenwire flap. Now she dives into the hedge, but Arthure has already hopped out and is crossing the garden toward the farm fields. Luckily the rabbit makes a detour to sniff some crumbs under the table where the Guets eat outdoors in fine weather. Laetitia crawls under the table and grabs her by the scruff.

Plumping down in a chair, she cradles the black bunny in her arms, scolding and kissing her at the same time. Zenda, her big sheep dog, who has been basking on the doorstep, plods over, seeking her share of attention. Zenda is heavy with the weight of the puppies she's about to have. Laetitia strokes her gently with one hand, keeping a grip on Arthure with the other.

Now about the Ardèche, she wonders. The trip will have to depend on when Mother returns from the weekly open market. Mother left in the early morning, carrying all her willow baskets. She will fill them with bargains. Usually prices are cheaper and fresh foods fresher in the markets. Farmers and fishermen bring their wares directly to the main square of a centrally located town. So do artisans and merchants.

Laetitia has often accompanied her mother to market. The vendors' sing-songs amuse her. "Regardez, regardez, 'sieurs-dames, j'ai des fines herbes de Provence. J'ai de thym, c'est bon, c'est beau." "Look, here, ladies and gentlemen, I have delicate herbs from Provence. I have thyme. It's beautiful, it's good." The vendor in the next stall sells spices from foreign countries. She is not about to be outdone by her neighbor. "J'ai du poivre de Cambodge, des épices excellentes et parfumées." "I have pepper from Cambodia, excellent and fragrant spices."

"Véritables occasions!" "Real bargains," sings the first, the tone of her voice mounting. "Ici aussi occasions!" retorts the second. "Here also bargains." Her voice rises even higher than her neighbor's.

6   Growing Up in France

Laetitia's mother pays no attention to the cries. She hurries from stall to stall, market list in hand. Laetitia often lags behind, giggling at the vendors' contests, eyeing stalls of candies and pastries, petting a pony whose master offers rides for children.

"Laetitia, Laetitia!" her mother is forced to call, and Laetitia slithers through the crowd to catch up.

"Laetitia!" Mother, home from market, is calling this minute. Laetitia returns Arthure to her hutch, this time firmly latching the flap. She parks her chewing gum on a convenient ledge near the doorway. Otherwise Mother will make her spit it out. Then she hurries into the rambling amber-colored stucco farmhouse, roofed in the tubelike orange tiles of southern France.

As usual, Mother has returned with loaded baskets. Laetitia helps unpack and put away. She smacks her lips as she lifts out a creamy Brie cheese, just ripe enough to ooze its yellow insides out of its chalky skin. Underneath she finds *quenelles*, sausage-shaped croquettes of—are these veal or fish? She sniffs one. Veal. Next, carefully, she fishes up a half-dozen small flaky pastries filled with glazed fruit: apple slices, peach slices, strawberries. "*Miam-miam*," she says. That's the French child's way of saying "yum-yum."

Just as the last of these goodies are stowed away, the grandfather clock in the dining room chimes noon. Father returns from the fields for lunch. Laetitia helps set it out in the garden. She carries a huge salad of home-grown vegetables, picked that morning. Mother follows with a casserole of zucchini. She had prepared the salad and the casserole before leaving for market. There is also a loaf of homemade paté, a velvety mixture of ground meats and liver, bound together with beaten egg and baked. Father brings out a bottle of wine for Mother and himself. Laetitia drinks water. French children almost never drink milk. As for wine, they are allowed a little, but only on very special occasions.

Two long, narrow loaves of French bread, crusty on the out-

Weekend Fever 7

side and cotton-soft on the inside, along with the Brie and other cheeses, complete the spread. A big bowl of sliced peaches will be brought out later for dessert.

As the family is about to sit down, friends arrive with a tractor part that Laetitia's father needs. They are invited to stay for lunch. Another bottle of wine and another loaf of bread are added to the table. There is more than enough of everything else. The Guets have many friends. Laetitia finds their frequent visits natural. The Provençaux are noted for warm welcomes.

Lunch is eaten one dish at a time; first the paté, then the zucchini, then the salad, then the cheese, and finally the peaches. The French spend much time, thought, and care on their cooking. They believe that the taste of each dish should be enjoyed by itself. Only wine goes all through the meal. Bread goes up to dessert time.

The wine is sipped slowly, sometimes along with water or mineral water. The bread, on the other hand, is devoured. Neither Laetitia nor any other French child could imagine a meal without lots of bread. Bakeries provide fresh loaves morning and night. There are never leftovers, not even from breakfast to dinner. Bread on the table is so important that when the French describe a very hard time, they call it "un jour sans pain"—"a day without bread."

Still, bread must be eaten properly. Laetitia eats it in the polite French fashion. She breaks each slice into very small pieces and tosses these into her mouth, one at a time. She bites into a slice only when she has spread cheese on it. Cheese is eaten on bread, not crackers.

The Guets take their time at lunch. At this hour all France is eating. Except in the biggest cities, stores have closed. Business has stopped. The roads are free of traffic. Not until between two and three o'clock in the afternoon will people finish eating and the country buzz back to life.

8 Growing Up in France

Partway through the Guet lunch, the grownups' conversation pauses. With her left hand, Laetitia puts her fork on her fork-rest, a small, footed bar, used to keep the fork off the table between courses. Eating with the same fork all through a meal leaves fewer to wash afterward. Laetitia holds her fork in her left hand, as do all Europeans. She never shifts it to her right.

Resting her fork and taking advantage of the grownups' silence, she asks whether mother could take her and Véronique to one of the Ardèche beaches this afternoon. The answer is yes—but not until Laetitia has practiced on her *flute à bec*. A flute à bec is a recorder. As soon as she has helped clear the table, Laetitia hurries to her practicing. Often she tries to put it off, but today is different. The sooner she's through, the sooner she will be splashing in the river.

Finally Laetitia Guet is on her way to the Ardèche River, after she and her mother picked up her friend Véronique. During the hour's drive, the two girls occupy themselves by inventing adventures for the dolls they have brought along. Véronique's doll meets an American boy in a *bistro* (a small, informal French restaurant). She goes to the United States with him and joins some cowboys. She and the cowboys discover hidden treasure in a desert. After fighting off Indians, they divide the treasure. Everybody is rich forever after.

The adventures of Véronique's doll come out of television and movies. American westerns and French copies of them are popular on TV screens and in movie theatres. Most children don't realize that these are stories of the American past. When they find out that there aren't any more cowboy and Indian fights, they are disappointed.

The girls tire of their dolls before they reach the river. They sing the rest of the way. Pont d'Arc, the spot they have chosen,

Weekend Fever 9

means arched bridge. At the far end of the stony beach the mighty river has carved an archway through a cliff so it can pursue its path to the great River Rhône and descend with it to the Mediterranean Sea.

Leaping through the arch, the river is in a rush. The children must be careful of the current. They dive in from flat rocks along the bank and paddle fiercely upstream. Laetitia feels herself being drawn downstream. She calls to her mother, who tugs her to shore. Laetitia dives in again, farther upstream.

She and Véronique would like to go canoeing. Downstream, where the river broadens out, the current is weaker. There canoes can be rented. Some families bring their own. They drive up in small cars with canoes lashed upside down on top. With their prows and sterns jutting beyond the car roofs at either end, they look like giant turtles. When a family arrives at its destination the parents and older children pile out and drag the canoe into the river while the younger ones dance around and squeal.

The afternoon is too far along for Laetitia and Véronique to paddle on the river today. Autumn mists are already rising as they scramble out of the water. Mother heads the car for home. As the sun fades, the children shiver. They wrap their towels tight around them for warmth.

After dropping off Véronique, they pull into the Guet driveway. *Tante* (Aunt) Nicole, down from Paris for the weekend, greets them.

"Zenda's puppies are here," she says.

Laetitia runs to the kennel in a courtyard at the far left of the house. There Zenda lived as a puppy. There she has had forty-five pups in the last four years. The new litter is black and tan, every one. Just like their mother. Laetitia counts them. Ten, in all. One is more roly-poly than the other nine. Laetitia resolves to keep him. His name is Oscar, she decides. The Guets will find homes for the others.

After supper she goes to the edge of a small woods and claps her hands three times. She is answered by three claps from the opposite edge. The claps are a secret code she has with a friend on a neighboring farm. Three claps mean I'll see you at the usual time. Two claps mean I'll be late. One clap means not tonight. As soon as the rest of the family has gone to bed, Laetitia steals out to meet her friend. She *must* pass on the news about Zenda's puppies.

THIS HAS BEEN A FINE DAY for Laetitia. It's been a fine day, too, for Antoine de Champeaux, who lives about two hundred and twenty-five miles north of her, in a region called Burgundy.

While Laetitia went swimming, Antoine took his tennis lesson. His instruction costs eighty-five francs in French money for twenty lessons. That's a little more than a dollar a lesson. Like Laetitia's swimming lessons, his are partly supported by the Secretariat of State for Youth and Sports. The agency pays the instructor's salary. The quonset-hut type of building that shelters the court is owned by the town of Autun, not far from Antoine's home. A town tennis club oversees the whole project.

Fourteen-year-old Antoine, wiry and fast on his feet, is one of the best players in his class. He practices between lessons on his tennis court at home. His class is all boys. Before the age of twelve, boys and girls learn together, but after that they are separated.

Antoine and his brother, twelve-year-old Dominique, live in what was once the gatekeeper's house at the entrance to a chateau, or castle. The old stone dwelling has been fixed up inside to suit the present-day needs of the family. The grandparents live in the chateau itself. Both buildings are tucked away in a thickly forested valley bounded by the Saône and Loire Rivers.

Father de Champeaux is president of the union of private

Weekend Fever 11

foresters in the District of the Saône and Loire. The members take care of privately owned forests—that is to say, forests belonging to lumber companies and in some cases to individuals with large estates. The many public forests of France are owned by towns and cities.

Father de Champeaux is also the Mayor of La Celle, a village near the chateau. The family is well thought of in the community, despite some teasing which the boys have to take from other children. They are teased about their grandparents' chateau and the "de" in front of their last name.

The chateau has been handed down in the family for generations. The "de" means that earlier generations of de Champeaux were lords and ladies. The other children in Antoine's and Dominique's valley come from simpler backgrounds. They are mostly sons and daughters of woodcutters, wood haulers, vineyard laborers, and cattle farmers. Their families have made Burgundy famous for wines and wood and white Charolais cows, with hides almost as woolly as sheep.

Woods, pastures, and vineyards are crisscrossed with rivers and the canals that connect them. On these Dominique sails a raft he has built for himself. Often he must pole around log-laden barges on their way to sawmills. He's used to such navigating. He has traveled as much as twenty miles at a time. His ambition is to sail on the Loire. For that journey, he is building a flat-bottomed boat.

Like a good many French children, Dominique is accustomed to making for himself the things that give him the most fun. When he was younger, he used to carve faces on chestnuts and exchange carvings with friends. Now, of course, he likes to watch the *télé*, TV, and he enjoys his electric train set. Sometimes he plays with his brother's auto racing set. Still, his raft is the most fun of all.

Laetitia Guet is the same way. She has a weaving board, wooden picture printers, and an automatic drawing slate. She has a game called Routes de France in which the players score by following the best routes from one region of the country to another. But all these stay on the shelves while she and her friend Véronique swing in a hammock they have woven from chicken wire and plastic clothesline. Or perhaps they camp their dolls in a tent they have put together from barrel staves and an old tablecloth.

While Laetitia practices her recorder and Antoine his tennis, Dominique sails his raft. Today's trip is short because there's a *foot* match he wants to watch on his grandparents' TV set. Though "foot" means football, the game is really soccer, which is played throughout western Europe. Besides hoping to return in time for the match, Dominique is supposed to catch a few fish for supper from the brook that flows through the de Champeaux estate.

The match begins before he reaches home. The team he's rooting for has won all the French national games. Today it's playing an English team. Dominique forgets the fish.

His mother, who half-expected he might, has prepared chicken, just in case. The family meal will start with soup, then they'll have the chicken, then a vegetable or salad, then cheese. For dessert, mother has made a flan, a custard served with caramel sauce. She sets five places. Augustin, the oldest son, who is studying law in the country's capital city of Paris, has come for the weekend.

At dinnertime, Dominique shows up in the jeans and T-shirt he had worn on the raft. His clothes aren't very clean and neither is he. Augustin, who is also wearing jeans, but clean ones, orders, "Go wash yourself and change your clothes." Dominique grumbles but obeys. Both he and Antoine look up to Augustin.

The family waits for Dominique by the fireplace, in which

hefty logs crackle. Misty September evenings, with heavy dew forming, are damp and chill in Burgundian valleys. The fire feels good. Antoine and Augustin talk in low voices. They are arranging to hunt together tomorrow. Antoine isn't supposed to hunt. He can't get a hunting license until he is sixteen. But Augustin takes him along as a helper. Antoine's mother and father don't know this.

The love of la chasse—the hunt—runs deep in the hearts of French males, young and old alike. On Sundays in the hunting season, rifle fire rattles from field and forest. The game is mostly small: rabbits, quail, thrush, bunting. But there are some larger prizes. Deer live in some of the forests, and wild boar roam some of the mountainsides. Augustin prides himself on the marksmanship he is teaching to Antoine. But he doesn't hunt just for thrills. "Kill only what you can eat," he insists. The de Champeaux will make good use of the kill. Families with small incomes and several mouths to feed count on the Sunday shoot as a budget-stretcher.

At dinner Father de Champeaux mentions quail he saw at the edge of forests he inspected that day. Antoine and Augustin exchange glances. Dominique reports on his trip. When everyone has finished eating, he and Antoine clear the table. The family moves into the living room. Mother works on some embroidery; Father sits down at the piano. He plays an old folk tune and Mother sings the verses. Everybody joins the chorus. Here is their song. It tells the story of a night watchman (*the chevalier du guet*), a member of a regiment called *marjolaine* (marjoram), who is patrolling above a paved riverbank (*quai*). A group of fellow-members (*compagnons*) of the regiment ask what he is doing out so late. He tells them he is searching for a girl to marry (*une fille à marier*). They ask what he will give her and he replies, "My heart" (*mon coeur*).

Compagnons de la Marjolaine

C'est le chevalier du guet
Compagnon de la marjolaine,
C'est le chevalier du guet
Gai ! Gai ! dessus le quai.

Que demande le chevalier ?
Compagnon de la marjolaine,
Que demande le chevalier ?
Gai ! Gai ! dessus le quai.

Une fille à marier
Compagnon de la marjolaine,
Une fille à marier
Gai ! Gai ! dessus le quai.

> *Qu'est-ce que vous lui donnerez*
> *Compagnon de la marjolaine,*
> *Qu'est-ce vous lui donnerez ?*
> *Gai ! Gai ! dessus le quai.*
>
> *Mon cœur je lui donnerai*
> *Compagnon de la marjolaine,*
> *Mon cœur je lui donnerai*
> *Gai ! Gai ! dessus le quai.*

Antoine and Dominique enjoy the old songs of their country as much as the modern ones. They also like American songs, especially rock and country-western. But when young people get together—on a hike or a bus trip, for example—almost always they sing more old folk songs than anything else. The de Champeaux keep singing until the boys' bedtime. Between eight and nine-thirty most French children between ten and fourteen are off to bed.

Saying goodnight, Antoine and Dominique address Augustin as *tu*, the informal way of saying *you* in French. Their parents call them "tu," but they call their parents *vous*. *Vous* is the formal word for *you*, also the respectful word. Children call their school classmates "tu," but their teachers "vous." These days in France adults use the "tu" with each other quite casually, but children are still required to say "vous" to them.

The two boys kiss their parents and brother goodnight, first on one cheek, then on the other, in the French fashion. After the goodnights the boys climb a steep staircase to their bedrooms. The hall clock strikes nine.

A VILLAGE CLOCK in the Vosges mountains, some two hundred and fifty miles to the northeast, chimes the same hour. More than two thousand feet above the village, fifty éclaireurs (boy scouts) and éclaireuses (girl scouts) have finished a supper cooked over butane gas. They used the gas instead of burning wood to avoid any danger of starting a fire in the pine and oak forest where they are camped for the weekend. Above them tower the ruins of an ancient castle, Frankenbourg. They will explore it tomorrow. Meanwhile, stomachs content, they roll up in sleeping bags inside their tents. Hanging from the ridgepoles are the guitars and recorders with which they accompanied their singing in the bus on the way from home. Home is Strasbourg, the capital of the region called Alsace. The bus had left them at the bottom of a trail just beyond the village. Then it was climb, climb, climb. They earned their good meal and sound sleep in the nippy mountain air.

Éclaireurs, éclaireuses. The French word is an army term for rangers, those who go ahead of troops to explore the lay of the land and the position of the enemy. Translated another way, however, it can also mean those who light the way for others.

Éclaireurs and éclaireuses don't have separate organizations or troops in France. Except for very young beginners, the equivalent of Brownies and Cub Scouts, boys and girls meet and work together. Usually, however, different tasks are assigned to each. For instance, the girls among the Vosges campers planned the menus and bought the food. The boys mapped the trail.

The French word for troop is *unité*. The Strasbourg *unité* calls itself Rotterdam, after a section of the city where most of the scouts live, many of them in a housing project. The patrols within the *unité* have also chosen names. They are the wolves, the panthers, the tulips, the lances, *l'orangerie*, Kléber, and Anne Frank. L'orangerie is a park in Strasbourg. Kléber was a famous general at the time of the French emperor Napoleon. Anne Frank was a Dutch Jewish teenager who hid with her family from the

Weekend Fever 17

Nazis during the Second World War. They were discovered and she died in a concentration camp.

The Rotterdam unité meets weekly. The boys and girls come to meetings in their everyday clothes—no uniforms. One can see that they are scouts, however, from their hats and the kerchiefs around their necks. The kerchiefs are green, bordered with white. They bear the symbol of the wearer's patrol. The hats are cowboy style, secured with an elastic under the chin. An éclaireur wears his tilted toward the back of his head. An éclaireuse slants hers over her right eye. They are so pleased with these hats that they often keep them on indoors.

French scouts take many trips. In one year the Rotterdam unité logged some two hundred and fifty miles on foot. In summer they visit other regions of France, sometimes other countries.

One summer they traveled by bus to Laetitia's region, Provence. They camped each night along the way. In towns and villages they filled their willow baskets with provisions and their jugs with water. When they reached Provence they set up permanent camp. Every day they hiked to a different point of interest, from ancient abbeys and ruins of Roman cities to modern dams and power plants.

Once they visited Rotterdam in Holland. They stayed in the homes of their hosts, a Rotterdam scout troop. They have sent representatives not only to scout jamborees, but also to international meetings of other youth groups in several countries. They have traveled in the Soviet Union and the United States. These longer trips are taken only during school vacations, but every other Sunday, all through the year, the Rotterdam unité members are off on some expedition, singing as they go.

Back home comes the hard work. They are required to make written reports of their experiences. Usually they illustrate these with the photos they have taken or with drawings. Sometimes they include dried leaves or flowers of the region. Here are some translated comments from a report on the visit to the castle of Frankenbourg. It was written by a combined team of wolves and panthers: Rose and Mochel Pascal, Jean Paul Ledig, Claude Veltman, and Thomas Lavaux. Rose, the oldest, was fourteen.

> In the earliest documents, one finds that a Roman camp was located here. . . . The present castle was begun in 1105 and finished during the first half of the twelfth century. . . .
>
> After 1232 the castle belonged to the governing council of the knights of Strasbourg. The administration of the city was conducted from the chateau. . . .
>
> In 1632, Jean Scherer, a high official, ordered the treasure of the council to be removed in advance of the arrival of the Swedish army . . . which had already conquered northern Alsace. . . . The army set fire to the castle. . . .
>
> The ruins of a round dungeon at the northern end of the courtyard and of a square tower at the southern end remain today. Also remaining are parts of the entrance gate, a triangular tower flanking the entrance of the ramparts, chapel and the lodgings of the guard. . . .

The report is illustrated by plans of the ruins and sketches of the ramparts and round tower, with measurements for each. It contains, besides, fifteen color photographs, two charts showing the lay of the land, and samples of eight different kinds of foliage

Weekend Fever 19

collected on the climb to the castle. *Édition Spéciale*, reads the label on the hard cover. The cover picture is a charcoal drawing of how the authors believed Frankenbourg looked before the Swedish army destroyed it. Their belief was based on their plans of the ruins.

The Édition Spéciale reported fun as well as serious work. The *Journal de Marche*, the diary of the unité's activities, was kept by Rose Pascal. She liked to record meals:

> At noon, each patrol made its own lunch. We dined on a meal worthy of Maxim's!

Maxim's is a famous and very expensive restaurant in Paris. Rose continued:

> At four o'clock, blessed hour for food lovers, we returned to camp for our afternoon snack. Castor, majestic as a king, awaited us.

Castor is the children's nickname for their scoutmaster. They named him after an imaginary hero of ancient Greece.

To help pay for their trips, the Strasbourg scouts put on shows, which are well attended. One of their most successful was a pageant set in the reign of Louis XIV. He was a colorful French king who encouraged some of France's greatest artists, architects, and writers. The scouts' re-creation of his times paid for several trips like Frankenbourg.

EXCURSIONS LIKE THE FRANKENBOURG weekend are a national habit. In all France, the weekend is country time. Laetitia and the de Champeaux boys are lucky. They already live in the country. City children like the Strasbourg scouts are lucky. A way is provided for them to reach the country.

Many have to find their own way. Groups of teenagers ride their bikes on day trips to the nearest field or forest, seashore or river bank. Sometimes they ride two, even four abreast, holding hands.

Other children travel with their parents in the family car. What a slow trip that is! Here an *embouteillage*, there an embouteillage, everywhere embouteillages. "Embouteillage" means "stuck in the neck of a bottle." That's how the French describe traffic jams.

The weekend before school starts in the fall, cars leaving and returning to cities are really stuck. French children go to school on Saturdays. They get off on Wednesdays instead. Therefore this chance is the last one, except for a few vacation periods, to spend a full weekend in the country. The homes of country people are full of city relatives for those precious days.

Sunday is often picnic day. The French picnic is a production. Folding chairs and tables are squeezed into mini-size cars, along with the children, the china plates, glasses and silverware, tablecloth, baskets of food, father's fishing rod or frog net, and probably the dog.

By 11:30 almost every desirable picnic spot is taken, especially alongside brooks. Church-going families have attended a service late Saturday afternoon so as to be free for an early start Sunday morning. Many churches hold Saturday services just so their people can manage that quick Sunday getaway.

In the chosen spot the car is unloaded. Boys help their father set up the table and chairs. Girls help their mother spread the tablecloth and set the places. The tasks of boys and girls are still distinct in France. Next comes the moment the children have been waiting for ever since they left their house. The food is unpacked. Nothing so slight as sandwiches or hard-boiled eggs. Picnic fare is as ample, with as many courses, as a meal at home. There

Weekend Fever

may be a *quiche lorraine* to start, which is an egg, ham, and cheese pie. Next a chicken or a platter of different sorts of spicy sausage, then a salad, cheese, and either fruit or tarts for dessert. Bread throughout, naturally, and wine for the grownups. At a picnic, children may sometimes have sodas instead of water.

After lunch Father goes off to fish or, if the area is swampy, to catch frogs. The legs are delicious, cooked. Older boys accompany him. Younger ones play ball, wade in the stream, or gather walnuts, chestnuts, and ripe purple figs in season and in areas where they grow. Girls help their mother pick wild flowers and wild herbs: fennel, thyme, and rosemary. These will be dried and stored in the herb baskets that hang on the kitchen wall at home. Depending on the time of year and the region of the country, they may also hunt wild strawberries and mushrooms. Everything that's caught or picked will be a welcome addition to the family larder.

As shadows lengthen all the finds are packed in the car. Patiently the family joins the returning *embouteillage*.

Families who live the farthest south in France, along the border of Spain, may make a day's spree pay for itself by crossing the border and returning with bargains. Prices of Spanish wines and food supplies are about half French prices. The two countries are separated by the Pyrenees mountains, over which there are a number of passes. Among the most popular is the pass at Mount La Rhune in the west. The northern slope of La Rhune is French, the southern slope Spanish. In Spanish shops at the crest, huge hams and giant jugs of wine sell for a song.

The ride up La Rhune is what children enjoy. A tiny train, open on both sides, spirals up a single narrow-gauge track. The train hardly ever starts on time. The conductor always waits for some late passenger. When he arrives and the train finally chugs forward, all the other passengers cheer. The conductor toots the train whistle to scare the shaggy, black-snouted, black-legged Pyrenean sheep off the track. Children baa at the sheep and neigh at ponies grazing in fields of fern. Three-quarters of the way up, a descending train waits on a siding. The people in the two trains wave and shout greetings to each other.

At the top, while their parents shop, children scramble among scattered rocks. From the highest rocks they can see the Atlantic Ocean far to the west. To the south and east, the jagged Pyrenees bite into the sky. To the north they can look down on the villages from which they have come, nestled in ravines that are beginning to fill with shadows. Already the daytime color of their mountains has begun deepening to beige. The train is tooting. Time to go home.

Lugging their hams and jugs of wine, everybody climbs aboard. The beige of surrounding peaks turns to peach, then lavender. Dribbles of cloud settle in the ravines below. Some of the hams are piled on the children's laps. They drowse over the load as the little train lurches downward into the dusk.

When young people can't weekend in the country, they amuse themselves in the city. In Paris, fathers and sons often fish in the River Seine, which swirls muddily through the middle of the city. They sit patiently on the paved banks, dipping their rods up and down and hoping.

In the Tuileries, a giant garden in the center of the city, children sail toy boats in a placid pool or play *joli lastique* in the shade of clustered trees. Joli lastique is a tricky form of jumprope. Two children step inside a circular elastic cord and move back from each other until they are about four feet apart. The cord, held around their ankles as they move, is stretched to a narrow, taut oval. Another child jumps over this oval. Then she jumps in and out again, with both feet. She repeats the in-and-out figure, but this time landing with one foot in and one foot out. The cord is lifted higher and higher while the jumping continues. When the cord is

Weekend Fever 23

at the knee level of the children holding it, a player who has reached this point without a miss has to land with both feet outside, one on each side of the cord. Only children who have practiced a lot can do it. To add to the difficulty, the two children holding the cord around their legs wiggle and shimmy so as to make the cord quiver and shake at this last stage.

The big attraction of a Sunday afternoon in Paris is the bird market. Almost as many children as birds are to be seen there. The children press around the cages, munching hot roasted chestnuts which their parents have bought from a vendor near the market. The children's chattering mingles with the cheeping, tweeting, peeping, and cooing of all sorts of feathered creatures: parrots and parakeets, canaries, doves, magpies.

Most of France's cities and almost all French towns have public swimming pools. Parks, not as big as the Paris Tuileries but just as pleasant, are tucked away in most city neighborhoods. These pools and parks are crowded with children on warm weekends. If the park walks are paved, the children bring their skateboards. Sometimes they even ride these in the streets and get in the way of drivers, who honk angrily. The skateboards are making the drivers slow down and miss green lights.

LIFE IS NOT ALL PLAY, even on weekends, however. Chores combine with fun to knit the pattern of family life.

Above: Laetitia Guet and her friend Veronique play in the hammock they made.

Above right: Arthure the rabbit joins Laetitia and Veronique and their Barbie dolls.

Below right: The Guet farmhouse, made of stone and stucco, with a red tile roof, is typical of buildings in the south of France.

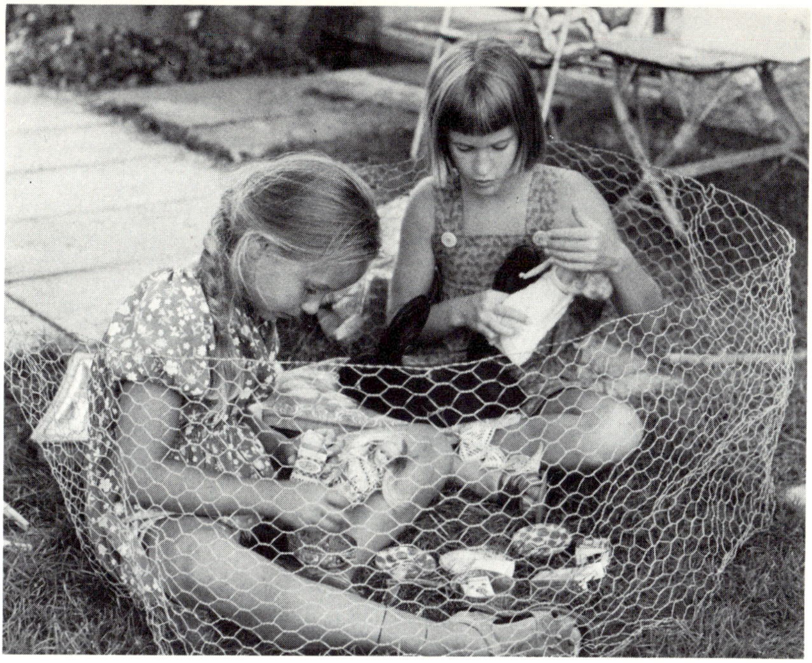

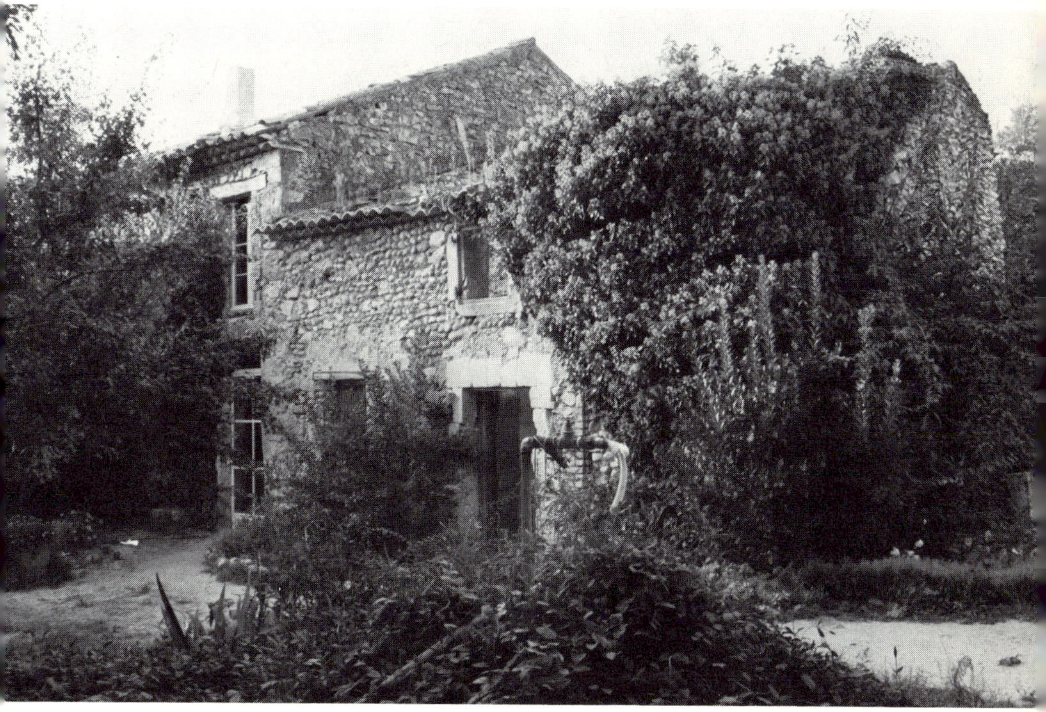

Antoine de Champeaux takes a tennis lesson.

The de Champeaux family enjoys dinner the French way, served one course at a time.

Antoine and Dominique have a difficult choice to make.

Above: J. P. Aptel or "Castor" is the scoutmaster of the Rotterdam troop of Strasbourg.

Right: A member of the Rotterdam troop on the weekend trip to Frankenbourg Castle.

Far right: The éclaireurs and éclaireuses prepare reports of the weekend visit.

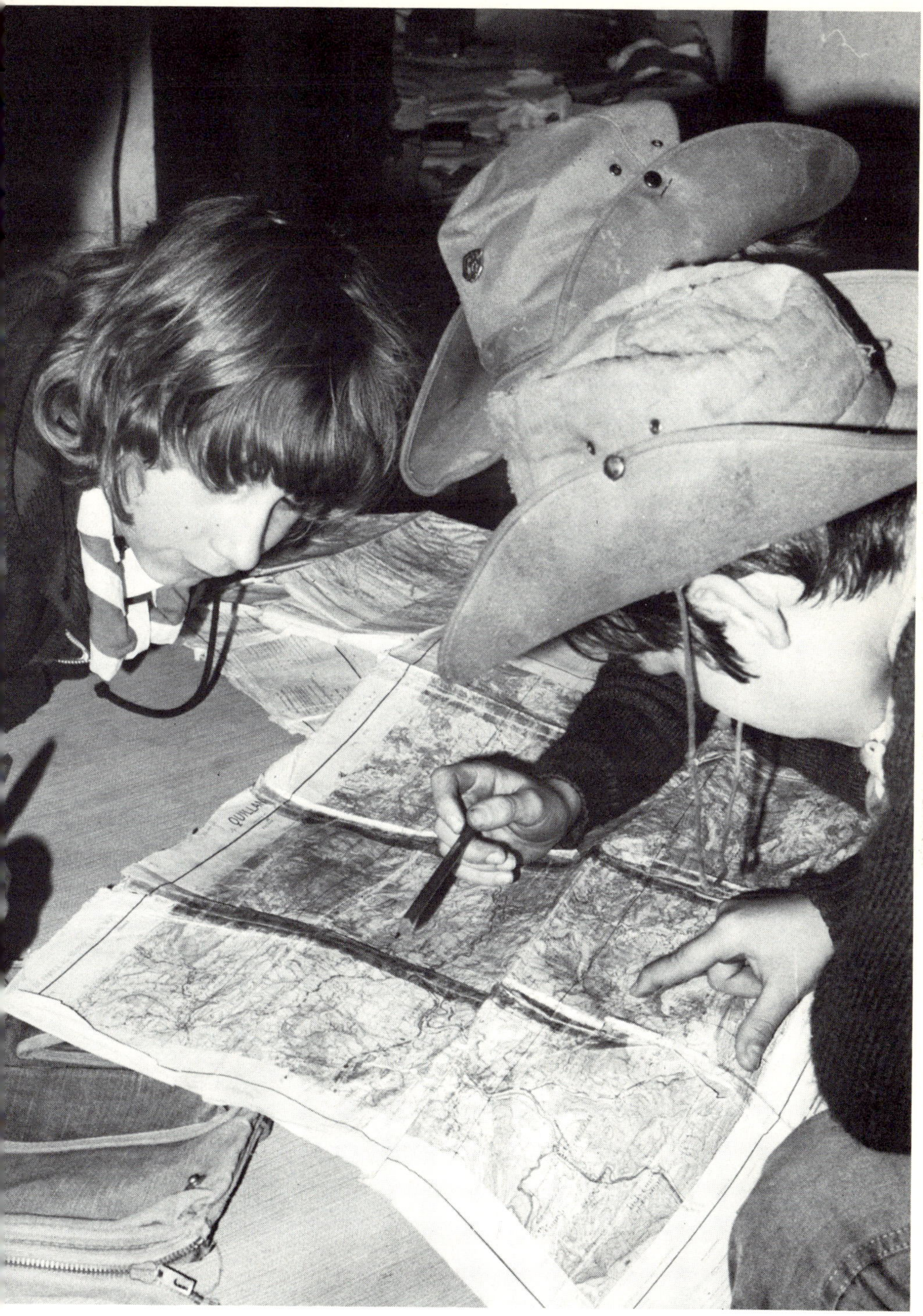

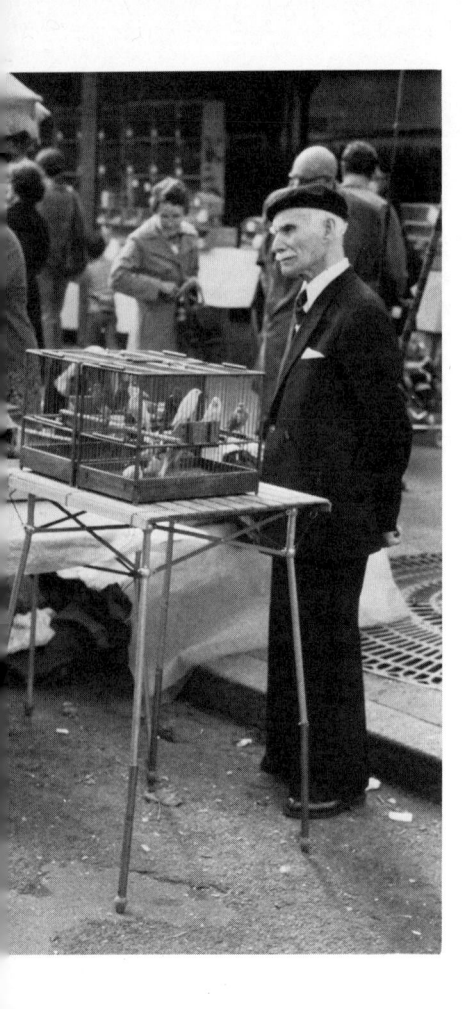

Old and young alike enjoy the Sunday bird market in Paris.

Right: Fishing in the Seine is a favorite weekend activity in Paris. FRENCH GOVERNMENT TOURIST OFFICE

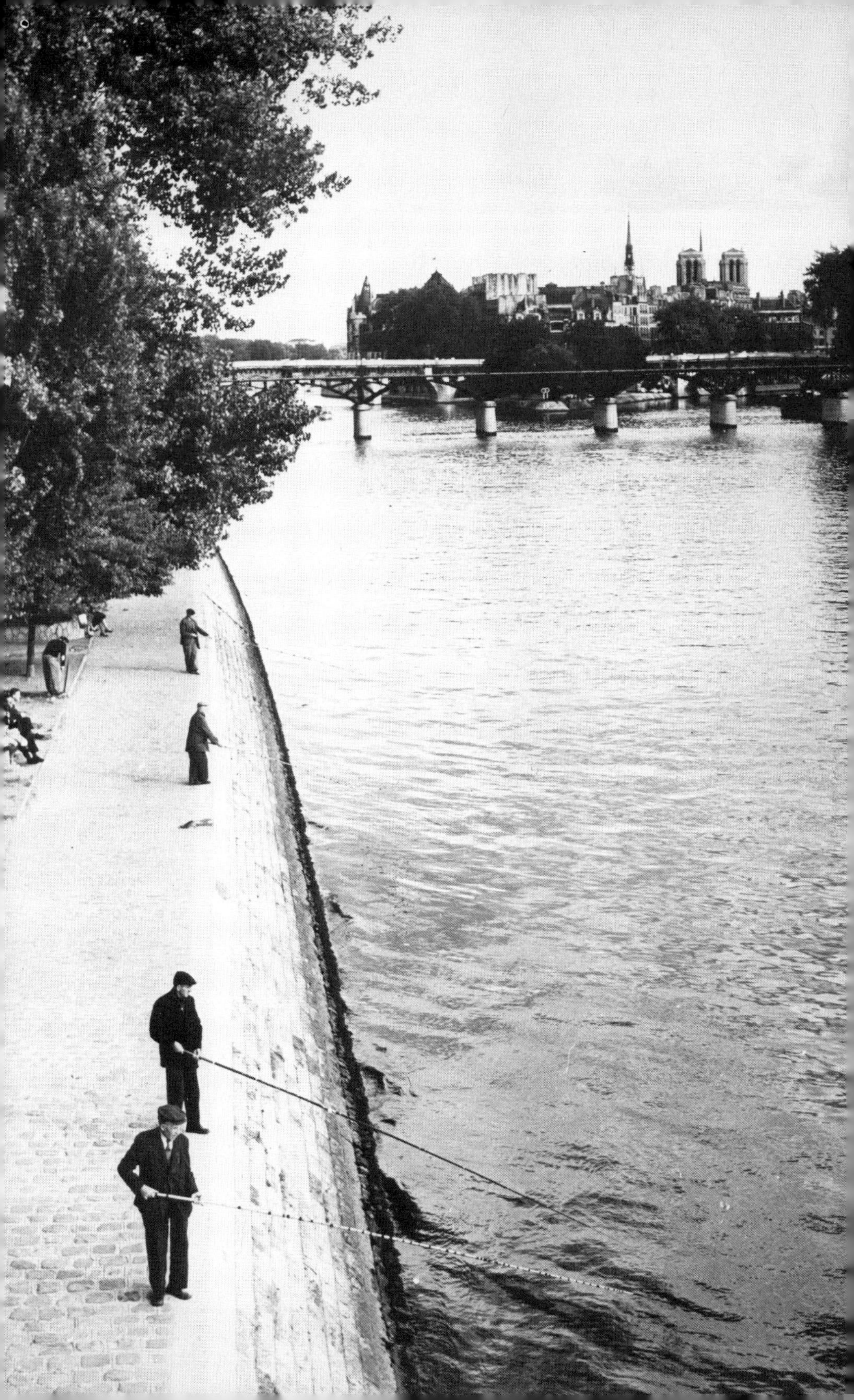

2
Families at Work

ALMOST ALL FRENCH CHILDREN are expected to help out around the house. They help inside and out. They garden, tend animals, sweep, shop, tidy, and set, clear, and clean up meal tables. In the Alps they cut and stack wood besides. Snow falls early, drifts deep, and stays late in that range of mountains in the extreme west. By the first of September families are piling the logs, which will provide winter heat, high around their homes. The deep overhang of the roof will keep the supply from being drifted over and prevent the snow from packing so tightly against the house that no door can be pushed open. Indoors will be warm and cozy.

Some children are called upon to give more help than others. If Mother is among the forty-one percent of French women who hold down jobs, girls in the family may take all the housework off her hands during school vacations. They also take care of younger brothers and sisters. The average number of children in a family is two or three. But in the country it's not unusual for a farmer and his wife to bring up five. Some older sisters have their hands full!

They don't have to do all the work alone, though. Boys help

Families at Work 25

out too. They wash dishes and mop floors. For a mop they tie a coarse cloth to the end of a stick and swirl it around. They call this a *serpillière*. Sometimes boys do the grocery shopping; sometimes their sisters do. "*Je vais faire les courses*," says the shopper "I'm going to make the rounds."

Make the rounds is right. Except on market days, when everything can be found in the town square, a shopper must go from store to store for the different provisions on his list. Bread comes from the *boulangerie*, bakery, meat from the *bûcherie*, butcher shop. Unless, that is, one wants coldcuts. Those, along with an assortment of patés, pre-cooked roasts, and other delicacies, are to be found at the *charcuterie*, which is even more tempting than a super-elegant delicatessen in the United States. If cheese is on the list, it may be bought in one of two places, an *épicerie*, grocery store, which also sells fresh vegetables and fruits, or preferably a *laiterie*, a dairy shop. Also fruits and vegetables should preferably be purchased at the *fruitier*, fruit shop. The épicerie, on the other hand, is the best shop for wines and of course for noodles, rice, sugar, flour, and other staples.

Don't worry that a French child on a shopping tour will be confused about where to search for what he's supposed to get. It's wholly natural for him to visit this store for that, and that store for this. Where else would one go?

His two favorites are the *pâtisserie* and the *confiserie*, the pastry shop and the candy store. If he isn't sent to either one, he will window-shop. Wistfully.

Some children live in areas where *supermarchés*, supermarkets, have opened. These are only in or near cities, large towns and nearby suburbs. They are not part of shopping centers. They are just markets, standing alone. But the *hypermarché*, hypermarket, is a shopping center in itself. It sells not only food, but also clothing, camping and sports equipment, quite possibly paint and hardware, probably furniture, and likely as not toys and knickknacks, among shelves and racks of other goods.

There's never more than one supermarket or hypermarket to an area, however. In small towns there are apt to be a couple each of the specialty stores except for the bûcherie, which lacks competition. In bigger towns and in cities there can be dozens of every kind of store. So while the French, especially young working couples, appreciate the convenience of the supermarché, they still do not want to lose the chance to compare prices and quality that the system of different shops for different foods provides.

Most owners of small shops know their customers. When customers' children do the marketing, a proprietor will look at the list mother has given them and direct them to the best of everything. Even four- or five-year-olds are sent to buy simple things like bread. Once in a while a child may drop the unwrapped loaf on the way home. (French food stores don't supply bags.) "Ooh-la-la!" the child exclaims, as he picks up and dusts off the loaf. If his arms are full, he may let his dog carry the loaf in his mouth. Mother does the same. Dogs' mouths are much cleaner than human mouths.

Thanks to monster trucks, food shops, both big and small, offer a tempting choice of delicacies special to various regions of the country. The trucks grind around hairpin curves in the mountains and edge through the narrow streets of old villages, as well as bowling along the highways. They are noisy and smoky, belching black fumes into the clean country air, but they are vital to fast transport, especially of products that need careful handling and won't keep long. Once these products were almost impossible to sample beyond the limits of the region that produced them.

IN A NUMBER OF REGIONS, the well-being of everyone depends on quick harvesting of a crop for which the region is famous. In

Families at Work 27

autumn, it's grapes for making wine. In the countryside along the German border south of Strasbourg, in parts of Burgundy, in the valley of the Loire River, which cuts across the north, in sections of Auvergne, which is the mountainous heart of France, in the valley of the Rhône, around the Atlantic coastal section of Bordeaux, and in much of southeast France, grapes are gold. From them more than two billion gallons of wine are produced, bottled, and sold every year. Their harvest becomes a family affair.

Children, parents, grandparents, and whole colonies of neighbors and relatives may work together to gather the precious clusters. Women and children help with the picking. Men do the heavier work. The picked bunches are dropped into plastic pails. The pails are emptied into baskets strapped to men's backs, or slung on poles borne on the shoulders of two men. The baskets are emptied into a crusher on a rectangular wooden cart. Sometimes a truck is used to haul the pressed grapes for long distances, but the wooden cart is still a very familiar sight on the back roads of the wine country.

Some years, autumn stays mild and the grapes ripen late; then fast work is needed to get all the grapes safely in before sudden frost. If necessary, children may be excused from school to help out.

FROM SEPTEMBER TO APRIL, oyster harvest time, children of oystermen along the Atlantic coast also work hard. The yearly crop of some thirty-five thousand tons of oysters can be worth up to thirty million dollars. Between five and six in the afternoon, women and children wait for the men to row home through canals leading from twenty-four thousand acres of oyster beds. The oysters that fill their boats look like lumps of mud. They have been gathered from silt deposited by rivers where they meet the sea. The combination of fresh and salt water, of warm river and cold sea, produces just the right temperature and mix of minerals that oysters need. The special taste and texture of the French oyster results from its growth in this natural environment.

When the harvested oysters are dumped from the rowboats, the women and children set to work with blades attached to sticks. They use these to separate the oysters from the concave roof tiles to which they have attached themselves. The tiles are placed in the oyster beds at hatching time. May to August. For about three weeks the young ones swim around. Then they fix themselves in the hollows of the tiles. After five or six years they are big enough to be harvested.

When all the oysters have been scraped off, the tiles are spread on the ground. After they have dried in the sun for several weeks, the children will scrape off the caked muck, making them as good as new for re-use. The work is rough on hands. Children soon learn not to cut themselves on sharp edges, but the exposure to wet and cold reddens the skin.

Oysters are also grown in the deep coves that the sea, thrashing inland, and the rivers, pouring seaward, have notched in the coast of Brittany. This part of France is a peninsula jutting out between the English Channel and the Atlantic Ocean. The waters all around it are rich with fish. Breton fishermen make good livings.

Breton boys often fish with their fathers. When the fleet of boats returns to port, they row the catch to shore. The boats are painted in brilliant greens, blues, reds, yellows, even purple. They have fanciful names such as *Rien Sans Peine*, Nothing Without Trouble and *Chacun pour Soi*, Everyone for Himself. They are a colorful sight, anchoring inside a high stone breakwater at sunset.

From each boat the fish are packed into cradle-shaped boxes, which are then lowered into the dinghy. A boy rows the dinghy to the foot of a long ramp on shore that descends from the fish depot to the water. A chain of men forms on the ramp. They heave the boxes of fish from man to man up into the depot. When the dinghy is empty it's rowed out for the next load. Although cranes for unloading directly on docks are now serving bigger boats, the little family-owned vessels are still important in Brittany.

Disasters always threaten a fisherman's livelihood. He keeps a sharp eye out for storms that can drive the fish far out to sea and wreck his boat besides. But the disaster he dreads most is manmade. Oil spill. In March 1978 the biggest oil spill in history hit the Breton coast. A huge oil tanker, three times the size of a football field, smashed apart on a reef. Some two hundred and thirty thousand tons of oil spread along one hundred and ten miles of Breton coastline, covering four hundred miles of ocean. Millions of dollars worth of fish, oysters, and other forms of sea life were killed. "Le printemps sera noir," the fishermen warned. "Spring will be black."

The French government and the American Oil Company, the tanker's owner, set to work to clean up the spill. Breton families set to work too. The men dug ditches above the high tide line and lined them with plastic. Into these they shoveled oil and refuse, including dead sea birds.

Boys and girls wiped rocks clean with rags or scraped them with putty knives. They washed the oil from the wings of birds that had survived so that they could fly again. But nobody could do anything about the plankton, the minute organisms on which fish feed. Only after new growth of this staple in the fish diet could Breton boys again row dinghies full of fish to shore.

BURONS ARE ALSO FAMILY WORK CENTERS. These are snug fieldstone cottages, with barns attached. They are nestled in the Massif Central, the mountainous spine of France, which ridges the region of Auvergne. Auvergnat cattlemen often migrate to them in the summer with their herds, wives, children, dog, cat, and other pets. Plus geraniums for cottage window boxes. Plus tubs of deep rose oleander for cottage yards. Plus an entire *batterie de cuisine*, all the pots, pans, and kitchen utensils needed for cooking.

Once the work was very hard. All summer long, families made cheese from the milk of cows and goats. Now they have life much easier. Instead of making the cheese themselves, they sell the milk to dairies that collect it by truck. The dairies resell the milk to cheese factories. The children have more time to gather the wild blackberries that thicket the slopes. Their mouths are often purple from the abundant juice.

Buron families still make some cheese, however, along with delicious loaves of rye bread. What they don't need for their own use, they sell to picnickers and passers-by. A trip to the heather-carpeted plateau where the burons squat in the sun is a popular summer pastime.

Eleven-year-old Eric Belledent is the son of a cattle farmer in Auvergne. He lives in Chavaniac, a village of ground-hugging stone houses that spirals up a foothill of the Massif. In the spring he helped plant potatoes. Now, on an autumn evening, he's apt to be digging potatoes for the family's dinner. When he has finished, he whistles for his dog, Zomba. It's time for the two of them to bring the cows back to the barn from pasture. The herd of two dozen cows is among the largest in France. Only five per cent of the country's cattle raisers have more than twenty cows.

The Belledent herd is twice as large as it was when Eric was five. The government helped pay for breeding more cows and for enlarging the barn to house them. Eric and Zomba go out from their village to surrounding fields. Eric rounds up the herd with a stick he has slashed from a tree on the way. Zomba helps, yapping at the cows' heels to get them into line. The animals lumber from the pasture to a narrow dirt road. Eric walks behind them, flicking the heels of slowpokes with his stick. A bell hangs around the

Families at Work 31

neck of the lead cow. Unlike most bells, this one is wider at the top than at the bottom. The shape produces a deep-throated tone. Eric would be surprised to hear the flat, almost rattle-like sound of cattle bells in the Pyrenees, or the silvery tinkle of tiny Alpine bells. Every region has its own bell for its own beasts. They are supposed to serve as a follow-me signal for the rest of the herd, but the rest of the herd doesn't always follow. Certainly Eric's doesn't. So Zomba races up and down the line, keeping the herd from straying.

After the cows are safely installed and milked in the long barn attached to Eric's house, he washes up for supper. The cheese course has all his favorites, the foremost cheeses of his part of the country: the squishy, mellow Saint Nectaire, the tangy Forme d'Ambert, and the Bleu d'Auvergne, which stings his tongue and throat. The stingier the Bleu, the better Eric likes it. He is on thirds with the Bleu when his mother says, "*Cela suffit, Eric.*" "That will do, Eric."

When supper is finished he watches an episode in a *feuilleton*—a television serial—about a little blonde horse named Poly. Poly is a good detective. With a band of children, Poly tracks down jewel thieves and recovers their loot. Tonight he retrieves a black diamond. Eric is quite ready for bed after the diamond is found.

Soon his outdoor life will give way to classroom walls. For all the children of France the *rentrée* is coming.

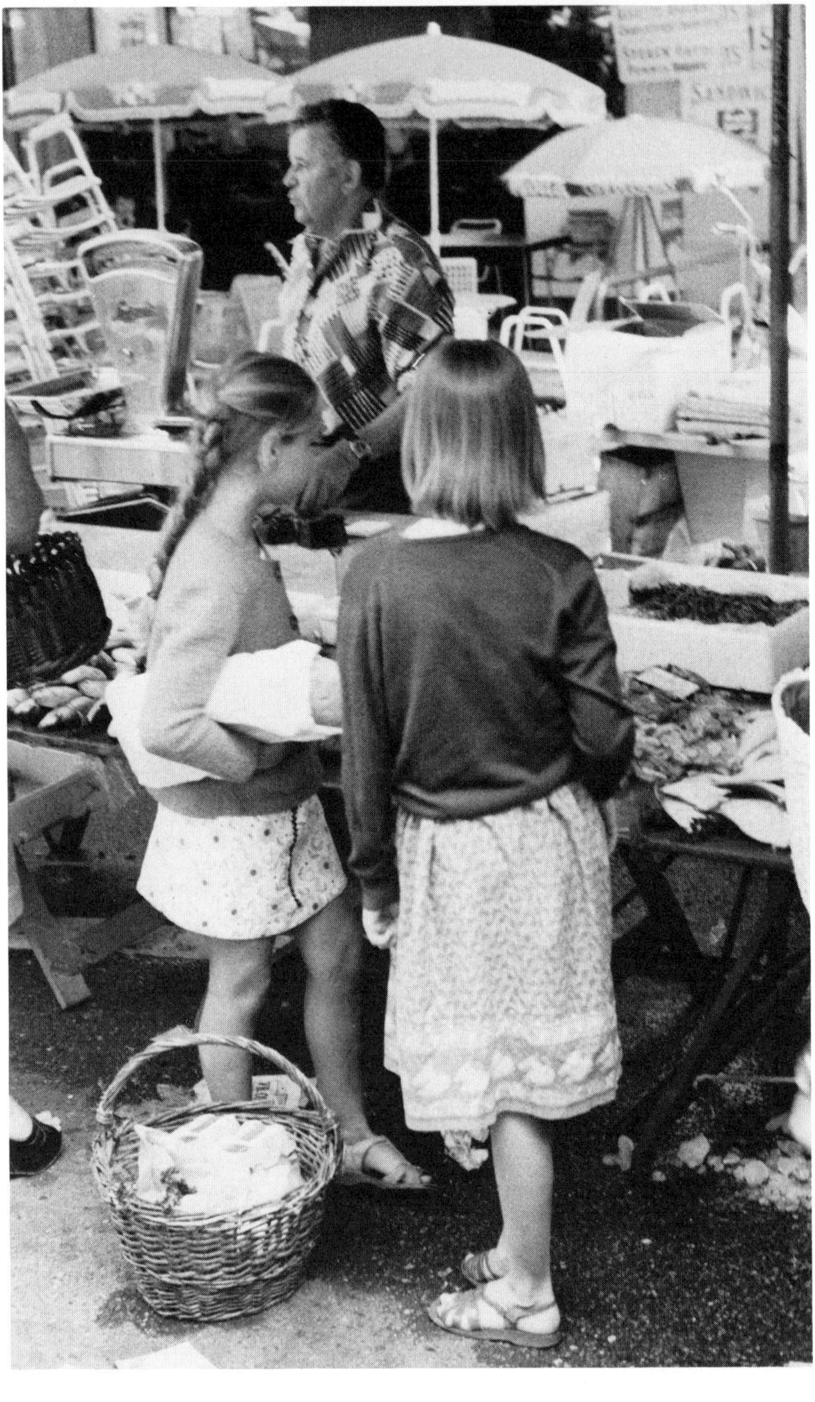

Far left: Laetitia and Veronique shop at the outdoor market.

Above: Laetitia tries out the tractor on the family farm.

Left: Young people help with the harvest in the grape-growing regions. FRENCH CULTURAL SERVICES

Oyster boats unload their catch at a harbor in Brittany.
AUTHOR'S PHOTO

A Breton boy holds one of the birds killed in the oil spill of 1978. LIASON/ANGELL

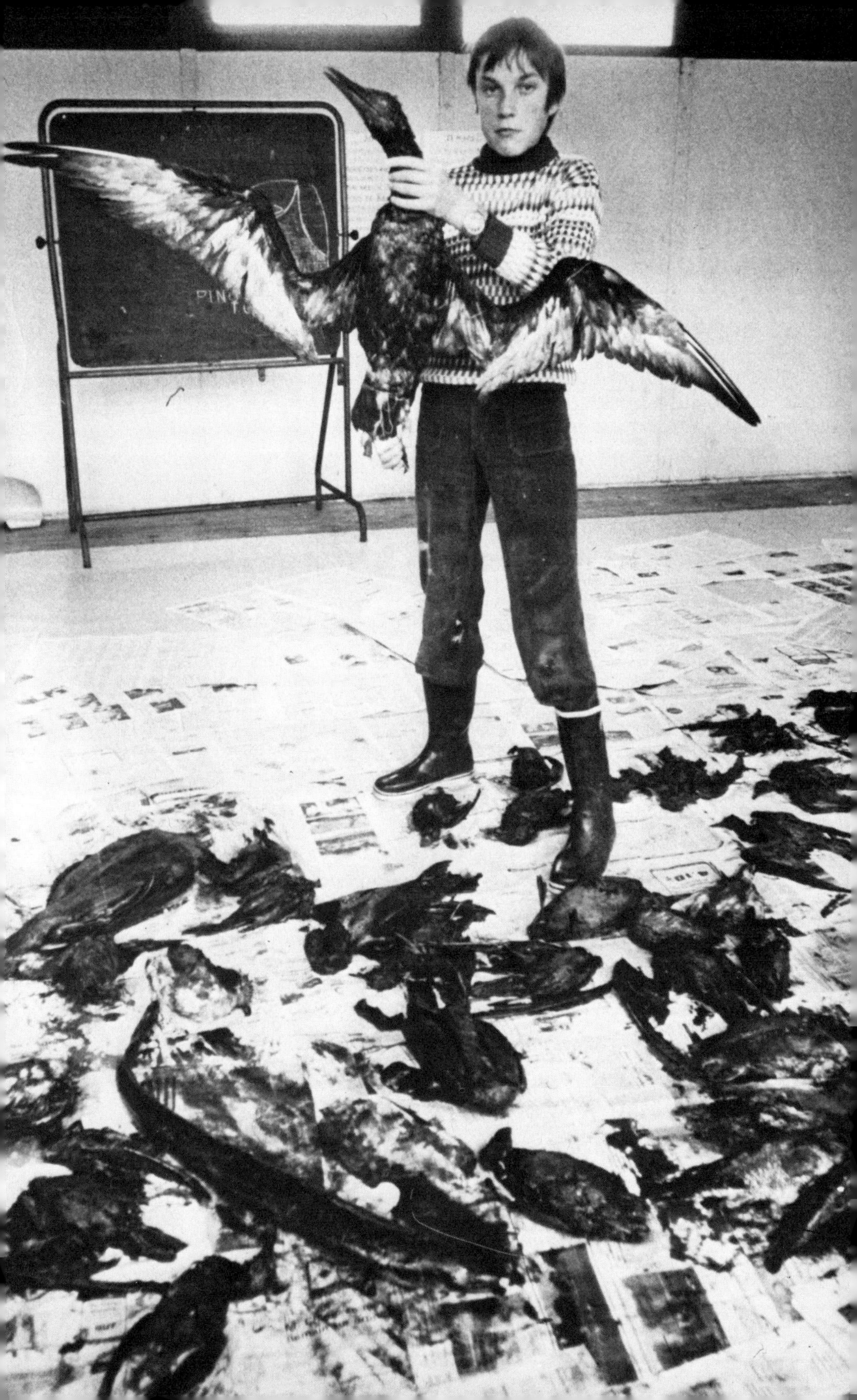

These girls play on the swing.

The boys prefer a rope ladder.

3
Welcome Back to School

"Joyeuse Bienvenue à Tous—Grands et Petits!"

"Joyful welcome to all—big and small," so reads the message on the giant blackboard on the school porch. In the surrounding yard, six or seven hundred young people, accompanied by parents, mill about. The girls wear blouses and skirts, or blouses and culottes, or blouses and jumpers. Their socks are knee high. Boys wear plaid or striped sport shirts and pants or jeans. Little first- and second-grade boys wear shorts. All carry brightly colored plastic briefcases for their books, notebooks, and other supplies.

Some of the children are sporting brand new outfits. For several weeks huge posters plastered outside stores have been reminding parents and children to prepare for the rentrée, the reopening of school. "Rentrée avec classe," the posters pun. French children could read the slogan two ways. Strictly speaking, classe means a class. But it can also mean style, as when, in English, someone is said to have class. The French borrowed this word from English. So the wording can be understood either as back to school with your grade or back to school in style.

Despite the advertising, by no means are all the children's

outfits new. A great many are made-over hand-me-downs from older brothers and sisters, even from neighbors. Families frequently exchange garments within a neighborhood. The exchange helps them cut the very high cost of clothing, especially children's clothing. In stores that sell moderately priced goods, a culotte for a ten-year-old girl can cost the equivalent of $40 in American money. A ten-year-old boy's sport shirt can nick the family budget for as much as $20. The older the child, the bigger the size, the higher the price. Obviously, children can't afford to be careless with what they wear. To protect their back-to-school outfits, new or made-over, they can buy smocks in the school lobby. Many line up to do so. Their teachers buy smocks too, to keep chalk dust off their clothes. In small country schools, women often tie pinafores over their dresses or slacks.

In the school lobby and in the yard outside, conversation buzzes. In the street beyond, horns honk as parents, toting children, tangle in a grand embouteillage. Most children must travel to and from school by whatever means they can manage. School buses operate only in the remote countryside, and then only where several small schools have combined into a central one that many students must travel long distances to reach. Elsewhere children ride their bikes to school, or walk, or take public buses, or are driven by parents.

As the last car rolls into the driveway, the school principal appears on the porch. She holds up her hands and the conversation ceases. The children form in rows in front of her. Their parents stand behind. The principal gives a little speech, welcoming pupils and explaining some changes in the school. A bright new wing has been added to the main building, now brown with age. She says she has tried hard to seat best friends together, but she hasn't always been able to arrange that. Desks in French classrooms are double; each pupil has a seatmate. When two friends have to be separated, the principal continues, there's no point complaining, "*on va mourir,*" "I'm going to die." They will probably live. Her audience giggles. Then she asks if the children are glad to be back in school. "*Oui,*" "yes," is the polite reply. It lacks enthusiasm.

After her speech, the children go to classes. Parents go with them as far as the classroom doors. Parents of tots just starting school may stay with them all through the first day. To these little ones school seems like a party. They have had the prospect sweetened with candies and cake. But ask more experienced pupils, in private, the question the principal asked publicly. The answer won't always be "oui."

Says Dominique de Champeaux in Burgundy: "I hate school. The day is too long. I'd rather fish or build my boats." Dominique has to leave home at 6:30 in the morning to reach his school in Autun by public bus. He doesn't return until six at night. His brother Antoine has a different opinion: "I don't enjoy it, but I want to get ahead. That doesn't arrange itself. I have to learn." Laetitia Guet in Provence agrees with Dominique. She hates being shut inside classroom walls.

Eric Belledent and most of his friends in Chavaniac's three-room schoolhouse are glad when the rentrée comes. For them the classroom is a place of adventure, a place where windows open on scenes beyond their pastures. Maps of faraway lands, works of great authors are like voyages of discovery.

In general children like Eric, who aren't used to meeting many strangers, enjoy the experience of school more than those who live in well-traveled sections. Teachers are not only leaders in adventure; they are friends as well. In remote villages they live in apartments attached to the schoolhouses. They are part of the village. They know every pupil outside as well as inside the classroom. School is like a second home—only more exciting.

A class may even keep pets. Classes in the two-room school at Colroy-La-Roche in the Vosges mountains keep rabbits and guinea pigs. They are caged just outside the building, so the children can care for them during holidays. Classes in the remotest areas of all, high in the mountains, may occupy the second story of a stable, with cattle housed below. There are fewer and fewer of these schools, however, as roads reach into the countryside.

Not all schools offer lunch, but country schools that serve several villages always do. At Glaine-Montaigut in Auvergne, three schools have been combined into a two-room school. At noon three dozen youngsters pile into the big kitchen, which also serves as a dining room. They seat themselves on benches at three tables covered with brightly patterned oilcloth. On each table is a basket containing four long loaves of just-baked bread. That's about seven slices for each child. They start immediately on the bread. It doesn't spoil their appetites. They go on eating heartily. There is soup and a steaming stew cooked that morning by the motherly lady who serves them. The stew is plentiful and delicious. The cheese is fresh and fragrant.

The dessert is a masterpiece that draws miam-miams from the children: huge apple *tartes*, two for each table. A tarte is a pie. The crust flakes into buttery crumbs as it is sliced and the apples drip a syrupy juice, aromatic with cinnamon.

Usually country schools like this one are more informal than city schools, but the children study the same subjects all over France. The national government directs education. As a rule, children must go to school from ages six to sixteen. In some special cases they are allowed to quit earlier. Also, if parents wish, children may start as young as two. Many parents do so wish. Some three million tots attend *écoles maternelles*, nursery schools. These have everything a small child could desire: gardens, swings and junglegyms, sand-boxes, and miniature autos to drive. The playrooms are stacked with toys. The nap rooms are comfortable. The dining rooms serve good food. If a child's mother and father both work, as is often the case in France, the école maternelle will care for him until 6:30 P.M.

When children are six, the time has come to enter primary school. Extra-bright children may start at five. In primary school they learn to read and write.

The style of handwriting has greatly changed in recent years. Once French children were expected to slant their writing to the right and add a great many flourishes. The result was pretty—but often almost unreadable. Now children are taught to write a plain, straight-up-and-down script that is clear and easy to read. It is also uniform. Everybody's handwriting looks like everybody else's. Here are two samples, written by two different children, stating the name of their favorite television program. Both like the *Wednesday Visitors* (*visiteurs du mercredi*) best. The first child has made a mistake with one of his accents. He's placed it over the wrong e at the end of *préferée*.

mon émission preferèe est les visiteurs du mercredi

mon émission préferée est les visiteurs du mercredi.

In primary school children also study geography, history, nature, and math. They learn the basics of the new math. They are given charts for multiplying simple numbers that are almost as handy as calculators. Here is one of them used by pupils in a primary school in the big industrial city of Clermont-Ferrand.

Perhaps the most difficult subject that children begin to tackle in primary school is the grammar of their own language. On this they have to work almost as hard as they would if they were

TABLE DE MULTIPLICATION									
1	2	3	4	5	6	7	8	9	10
2	4	6	8	10	12	14	16	18	20
3	5	9	12	15	18	21	24	27	30
4	6	12	16	20	24	28	32	36	40
5	10	15	20	25	30	36	40	45	50
6	12	18	24	30	36	42	48	54	60
7	14	21	28	35	42	49	56	63	70
8	16	24	32	40	48	56	64	72	80
9	18	27	36	45	54	63	72	81	90
10	20	30	48	50	60	70	80	90	100

learning a foreign one. In fact they have to master much the same rules as a foreigner does when he studies French.

THE STUDY OF FRENCH GRAMMAR is continued in a school called a *collège*. Don't mistake this for a college. Rather, it's like a junior and senior high school under one roof. The first two years are junior high. The next four are senior high. In these years, primary school studies are deepened and broadened. A magnifying glass is placed upon the workings of the modern world, its economics, technology, and languages. Roots in the past are brought to life. Art, literature, various sciences, advanced mathematics, and languages complete the subject matter. In the first year young people must begin to learn English. Later they may add another foreign language if they wish. Many choose German.

In Pertuis, a medium-size town in Provence, the German teacher travels from school to school to teach the language. She always brings Rudi and Trudi with her. Rudi and Trudi are puppets. They carry on lively conversations—in German of course. She also brings German comic books. After reading an episode in the book, the students choose classmates to act it out. The actors perform well and the class applauds heartily when they finish.

The comic book—the *bande dessinée*—is widely used in French schools to teach all sorts of subjects. Sometimes students are given assignments to make their own comic books instead of writing compositions.

Teachers also rely on records to add spice to studies. Records dealing with various subjects are part of the library of many schools. Children borrow them to play at home, just as they borrow books to read. Records are especially used for learning languages. Saint Martin's School, in the large old city of Montpellier in southern France, assigns records as homework in English courses. The children have a brightly illustrated textbook that describes two families, the Grays and the Millers, who live with their children and their dogs in the suburbs of London. The records dramatize the story in the text. Listening is the sort of homework young people wish more teachers would give! Naturally, they learn their English with the accent they hear from the British performers on the record. Like most western Europeans, the French speak English as the British do.

Welcome Back to School 39

When students reach their second year of collège, at the age of twelve or thirteen, they face one of the most important decisions they will ever have to make. It is one that will affect their entire future. They must decide what they want their education to train them for. Do they want to be prepared for jobs that require skillful hands? Or do they want to work mainly with their heads? If they hope to become mechanics, construction workers, machine operators, hairdressers, electricians, plumbers, carpenters, they will take one set of courses. If they aspire to the work of doctors, scientists, social workers, teachers, lawyers, economists, government officials, journalists, architects, or wish to continue studying for advanced degrees, they will take another set. They are at a turning point.

About forty-five per cent of French school children these days prefer to prepare for working with their hands. After collège, they will go to a Lycée d'Enseignement Professionel, or LEP. A lycée, which is the next step after collège, is the equivalent of a junior college plus in the United States, depending on the kind of courses the lycée offers and the number of years needed to complete them. An LEP, which teaches manual professions, gives three years of stiff training for the jobs students seek. LEP graduates are eagerly sought after by employers. When they graduate they are almost sure to get well-paid work.

Others, who seek professions that require training the mind instead of learning manual skills, go to lycées that specialize in teaching basics for the careers they have selected. Some go to classical lycées that don't prepare for any special career. They concentrate on literature, language, history, arts, and sciences. These students will specialize at universities later on.

The lycées are crowded, because there aren't enough of them. In recent years the government has been building more and more new collèges, but very few lycées. With some exceptions, they are not only crowded but dismal. Imagine a child who comes from a collège where he is accustomed to walking down corridors on whose turquoise walls hang paintings of scenes of his region. At La Grande Motte, a development of modernistic apartment houses bordering the Mediterranean, the paintings on collège corridor walls are of galloping wild horses. The children have visited these in a neighboring government preserve. They enter their classrooms through bright red doors. The classrooms are full of light. Plants grow in pots on the broad windowsills. Goldfish swim in a bubbling tank. The bottom is lined with fan-shaped shells the children have brought from the beaches. A baby turtle may be crawling over the shells. A student climbs or descends spiral staircases of wrought iron to get from floor to floor.

This same student enters an average lycée. Imagine his shock on the first day as he looks around and sees one shade of brown after another. He is boxed in by buff walls and ceilings, relieved only by chocolate-colored woodwork. He climbs creaking brown stairs. He walks down corridors paved with worn, dull asphalt tile. His classroom is packed; the windows are small. Most of the time, the class works under artificial light.

Worst of all, he may have to board in the lycée dormitory several nights a week. Lycées are located in towns and cities. Country young people who must travel long distances to reach them customarily stay overnight on Mondays, Thursdays, and Fridays. Collèges are also often located in towns and cities. Laetitia Guet will board three nights a week when she goes to the nearest collège, in Bourg-Saint-Andeol. But her environment is apt to be far more pleasant there, as the collège is new.

The relatively few new lycées are of course just as bright and attractive as any collège. Some, like the lycée Anna de Noailles in Evian on the banks of Lake Geneva, are even more so. The girls' dormitory is a small chateau. The boys' is a chalet. Located just across the lake from Switzerland and not far from the borders of Germany and Italy, the lycée accepts qualified students from these countries as well as from France. On a table in the well-stocked library lie current issues of magazines in French, Italian, German, and English, as well as publications of the United Nations. Most unusual of all, not only for a lycée but for any school in France, Anna de Noailles offers outdoor sports, including swimming and boating.

French schools are not strong on extracurricular activities. There are no school glee clubs, drama clubs, Little Leagues, or football teams. These are the affair of the Secretariat of State for Youth and Sports. That agency more than makes up for what the schools lack in the way of recreation. In cooperation with community groups, it offers many kinds of programs. These range from sports such as Laetitia's swimming and Antoine de Champeaux's tennis lessons to folk dancing, movie making, stamp collecting, newswriting, playing in orchestras, and dozens of other ways for children to be creative.

Especially at the lycée age, when school work becomes heavier, it's a welcome change to get away from it all on Wednesday and join in one of these pastimes. Exams come at the end of three lycée years, when students are seventeen or eighteen. There are two kinds of these exams. The *baccalauréat*, called the bac for short, is the harder of the two. The *brevet* is easier.

The bac is a young person's passport to any university in France, except for five which the French call the Grandes Écoles, the great schools. They are like universities called the Ivy League in the United States. They are even harder to get into, however. A student who hopes to make one must remain in the lycée for several more years.

Until recently the bac posed questions about all subjects taken in all previous years of school. Now the questions deal only with subjects the students have specialized in at their lycées. But it's still tough.

The simpler exam, the brevet, is a passport to business schools. The important difference between the two is that the bac opens doors to management careers, the brevet to workers' jobs.

From the lycées, then, a student goes on to a school or university where he will spend two to four years working for a final degree. Depending on what sort of training he chooses, he may be anywhere from twenty to twenty-five when he graduates. If he wants to become a lawyer, doctor, teacher, or other skilled professional, requiring special knowledge, he will take still further preparation.

Suppose a youngster doesn't want to continue at all. What about a girl like Laetitia or a boy like Dominique who hates school? Must they stay on anyway? No. After graduating from a collège, they can receive a *petit diplôme*, a little diploma. It certifies that they have been permitted to leave school and entitles them to return later if they wish. They are also offered the opportunity to work as apprentices in a trade and so learn by doing.

Up through the lycée, French education is free. At universities, students pay very moderate fees. The government pays the rest—besides giving full scholarships to about a quarter of the students.

During all their years of study, bright, medium-bright, and not-so-bright students are supposed to work together in the same classrooms. To teach them separately is against the law. Teachers complain bitterly about having to teach slow, fast, and average learners at the same time. Some even find ways of getting around the law, because they are afraid of boring their quick students or else not getting through to their slower ones. But the children seem to be neither bored nor lost. If they are aware of differences in the class, they simply disregard them. In schools where the rule

Welcome Back to School 43

is followed, it's a tribute to both children and teachers that they manage so well.

The rule against separating children according to intelligence is called the *loi* (law) Haby, after the French Minister of Education, René Haby, who conceived it. His decree was put into effect in 1977. Legal contests followed, but there seems little prospect of any retreat from an arrangement that is meant to create in the classroom the mixture of minds that children must meet in life.

The law also made other important reforms in French schools. It did away with a system under which teachers decided in a student's first year of collège what kind of education he or she should receive thereafter. The teacher's decision thus determined the whole pattern of the student's future life. Some were chosen to take courses that would qualify them to be managers or professional people; others were assigned to preparation for hand labor. A student's family could appeal the decision, but few did. Now it is the students themselves who, with their families, make the decision about their studies and their future.

Farm children were especially slighted under the old ways. They attended agricultural collèges that taught only farming. They learned nothing of the world in general—past or present. Four out of five dropped out of school at the age of fourteen. "We knew nothing. We felt like strangers in our own country," says one who was the product of that system, Jean Chrétien. He grew up to be a successful activist in the fight for broad education for farmers' children.

Today Eric Belledent has what Jean Chrétien fought for. He wants to be a farmer when he grows up, but he will not feel like a stranger in his own country. He will have a general education as well as a special education in agriculture. He can even take a bac in agriculture if he chooses. Once the bac was given only in classical subjects; language, literature, arts, and science. Now it is given in seven vocations as well.

Not everyone is pleased with such a change. "The bac doesn't mean anything any more," some grumble. The grumblers are living in the past—before 1968, that is.

In that year, French university students barricaded the streets of Paris. Singing the French national anthem, the "Marseillaise," they started a riot which turned into a nationwide revolt. They sought reforms in education.

The reforms have been slow in coming, but the loi Haby is, in part, a result of that youth crusade. Other groups with other aims joined the crusade. Since then the whole country has been quietly changing, and the schools with it. An air of flexibility is blowing through the classrooms. French schools are changing from what-always-was to what-is-to-be.

Desks in the always-was kind of classroom were nailed down in straight rows in front of the teacher's desk, which stood on a small platform. The teacher did most of the talking. Children spoke when called upon.

Desks in what-is-to-be classrooms are arranged sometimes in half circles, sometimes facing each other, or in whatever fashion makes the room most comfortable. The teachers' desks are at the same level as those of the students. Teachers put their desks where they please. They spend little time sitting, anyway. They move around the class, asking questions, lending a helping thought where needed. The students do most of the talking. The teachers make few statements. They ask questions. Sometimes they write something on the blackboard that they know is wrong. Then they ask the pupils for corrections.

In a new collège in Pertuis the class of Jean-Claude Soulié is working on a model of a Roman military camp. The camp grows daily. The children have reached the year A.D. 1000 in their study of Roman history. The model is being built bit by bit as their research reveals how such a camp would have looked in that year.

Monsieur Soulié, whom his students call the Prof, is assisted by class officers, elected by the class. There are two chiefs, a boy and a girl, and two subchiefs, another boy and girl. Any one of them can be asked to resign—not by Monsieur Soulié but by a class majority—if their leadership is found lacking. They are supposed to help keep work on the move. The children like to feel that the Prof and they are moving along together.

In some schools, periods are set aside in which students can discuss their feelings about their school and raise questions about why this or that has to be done and this or that can't be done. Such questioning would have been considered rude in old-fashioned French schools.

From the youngest grades up, there's a great deal of reading out loud. Where once the teacher did the reading, now the pupils do. Every child wants to be sure to get a turn, so a flock of hands go up even before the one who is reading has finished. That one pays no attention to the hands, being caught up in what the author is saying.

French students like to read to themselves, too. They make good use of their school libraries, both in and out of school. In small country schools, the books are kept on classroom shelves. The pupils are so familiar with them that they know just where on what shelf to find the books they need to answer their questions. They don't have to ask the teacher.

They especially like the television hours in school. The Ministry of Education operates its own television network. Teachers are given materials to prepare classes for programs and for discussing them afterward. The programs cover just about every subject imaginable. There are series on nature lore, on learning English, on art, science, music, geography, the theater, problems of modern living, history, literature of the past and present, and on and on. More every year.

But in spite of the students' enthusiasm, these programs are not always used. In fact they are used by just under half of the schools in France. Interestingly enough, that's about the number of schools where students have the good luck to be taught by up-to-date teachers in up-to-date buildings. These are the schools that have already reached the future. The rest have a way to go.

More public than private schools have modernized. The subjects taught in private schools are the same as those in public schools, but the way they are taught is often, though not always, more formal. Almost all private schools are run by the Roman Catholic Church. The French government offers to pay some and sometimes all of their expenses if they agree to follow government regulations. Practically all of them do agree. Fewer and fewer students attend them, however. At the end of the 1970s, not quite two million of France's thirteen million school children studied in private schools.

In public or private, city or country schools, pupils settle into the routine of learning as autumn gilds the land. After school, homework comes first. Rarely is it burdensome; French schools stress classwork more than homework. But parents insist on no play until lessons are done. Some parents, like Laetitia Guet's father, sit with their children during homework time, helping out with assignments if need be. Laetitia fidgets, chews her pencil, and bends over to pat Zenda and puppy Oscar, who are stretched out at her feet. "*Allons,*" says her father, "let's get going."

Laetitia will not watch television on schoolday nights, nor will Dominique, Antoine, Eric, the Scouts of Strasbourg, and most other French children. Parents generally prohibit it. The children must be in class by 8:00 or 8:30 the next morning. They must be clean and dressed and must have had their breakfast of hot choco-

Welcome Back to School 47

late, bread and jam or bread and thick, sugary honey by an early hour.

But wait till next Wednesday afternoon. The *Visiteurs du Mercredi* are coming!

Eric Belledent is happy to be back at school.

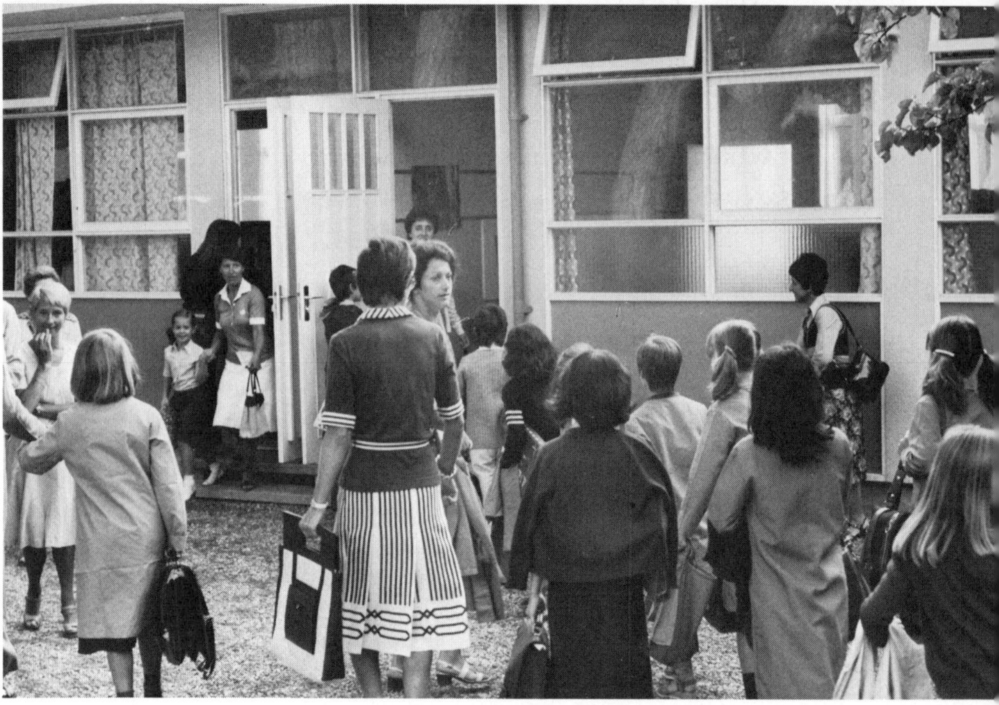

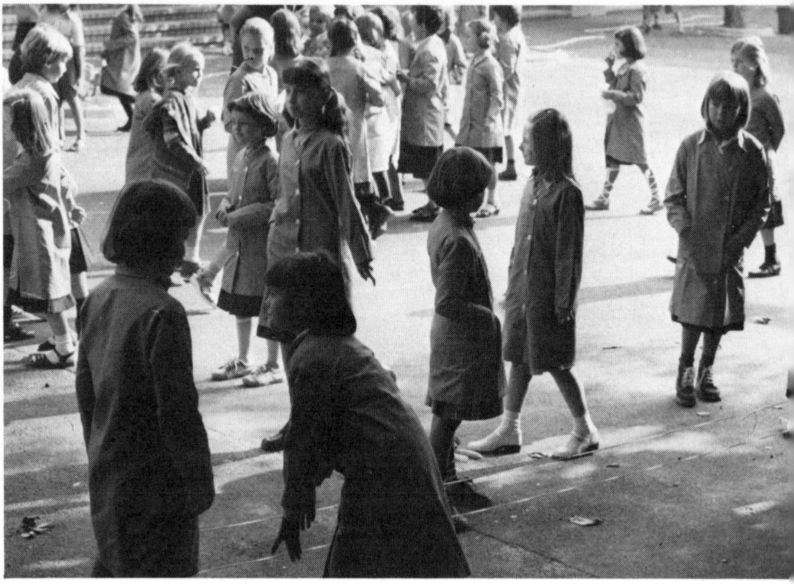

Above right: Rentrée at Ecole Sainte Thérèse, Montpellier.

Below right: These girls are wearing smocks to protect their clothes.

Above: One of the students and one of the pets at the two-room country school at Colroy-La-Roche.

Students at this country school are served lunch.

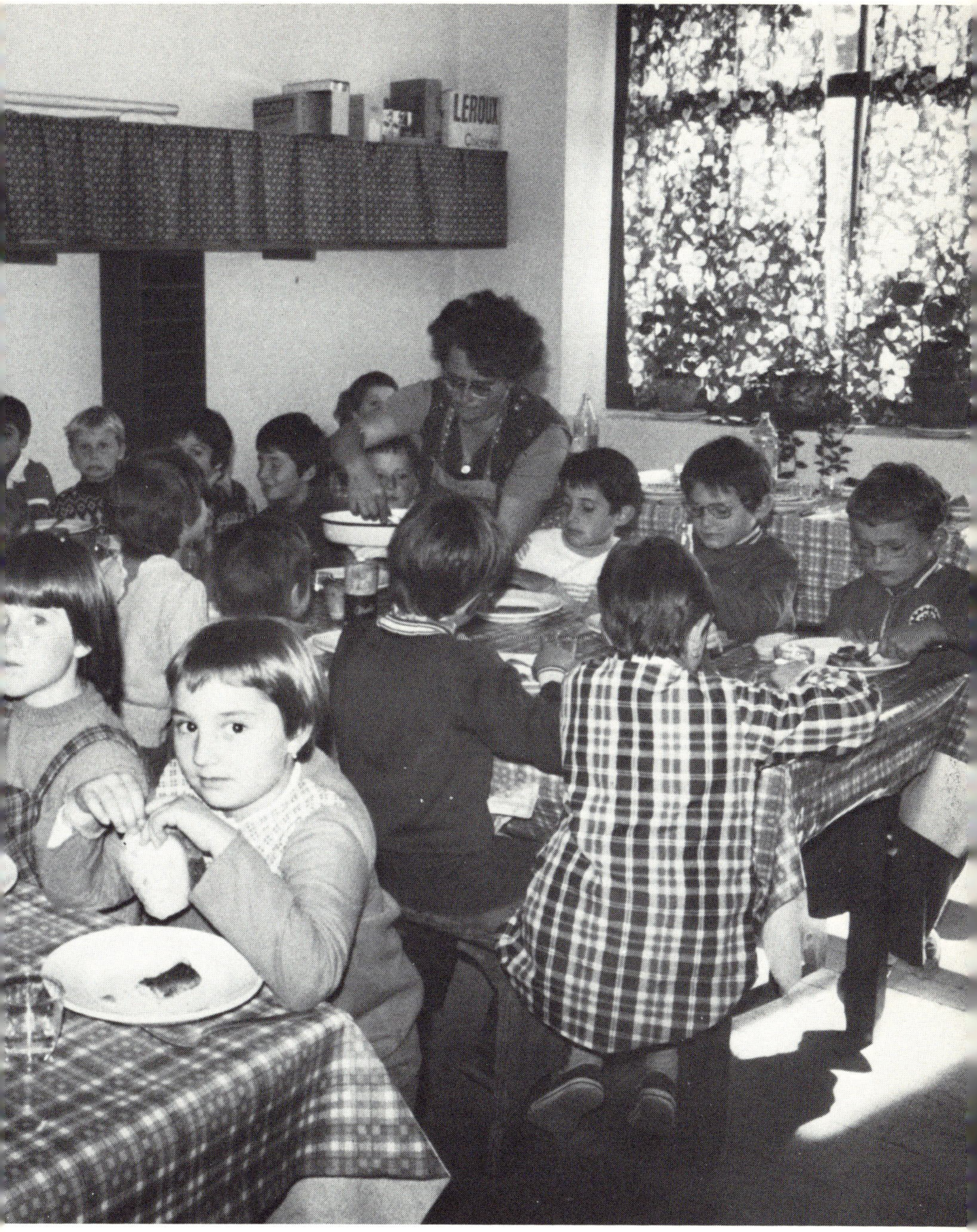
LEROUX

A teacher helps some of his students at the school in Colroy-La-Roche.

Monsieur Soulié with his class at the Collège Marcel Pagnol in Pertuis.

Older students learn grammar by playing a word game.

Students' bookbags are lined up before classes at the Collège Saint Paul on Corsica.

4
Winter Specials

On Wednesday afternoons from 1:38 to 6:07, the Wednesday Visitors drop into the homes of about fifty-seven per cent of French children between the ages of six and fifteen whose families own television sets. Eighty per cent of their families do.

Les Visiteurs du Mercredi is the most popular of all French children's TV shows. No one watches all afternoon, however. Different portions of this well-loved variety show are meant for children of different ages. The first episodes are for six- to ten-year-olds. A second set is for the older group, and the last hour and a quarter has something for everyone.

Here's a typical Wednesday on *Les Visiteurs*. The program opens with a cooking session: easy but delicious recipes explained in simple terms by famous chefs. Then a puppet show. Next a story about a gorilla. More puppets. Fifth on the screen is *La boîte aux Idées*, the Idea Box. It consists of letters from listeners, jokes, and a demonstration of magic tricks that children can perform themselves or with friends. Music follows: a lilting folk song. After that a serial about a pirate, one of several *feuilletons* or serials, on *Les Visiteurs*.

Reviews of new books, records, and sometimes films occupy

Winter Specials 49

the next spot. They are succeeded by a health series, La Vie en Toi, the Life Inside You. The program continues with a commentator's answers to the letters from listeners read earlier during the show. Two feuilletons bring us to the end of the first section. One is the story of a kooky cat, the other a translation of the novel Swiss Family Robinson, by a Swiss author and his son, Johann David and Johann Rudolf Wyss.

The second section, Le Club des 10–15, has much the same pattern, but the tone is teenage. A series on American rock music includes rock history along with performances by popular American rock musicians. Folk songs alternate with modern ones. A magician explains his magic. There's a feuilleton about robots. Then sports.

The mixed section is given over to cartoons, news stories, and features such as the many uses of the bicycle in France, from mail delivery to Le Tour de France, which is an annual round-the-country bicycle race. There's a cowboy or policier, detective, drama. Finally comes the most eagerly awaited half hour, the feuilleton Zorro. This Walt Disney production is a rousing adventure story set in California in the days when it was a Spanish colony.

A close second in popularity to the Visiteurs is a late Saturday afternoon show called Restez Donc Avec Nous, Stay with Us. Samedi est à vous, Saturday Is Yours, and Rendezvous de dimanche, Sunday Meeting are farther down the scale of favorites. All four have the same variety format, but Les Visiteurs seems to have captured the keenest interest.

Perhaps the reason is Christophe Izard. He's the young man who created and directs this program. He has his own philosophy about TV for children and his work reflects it. "French children," he says, "automatically think they are at fault when some mishap occurs. There are youngsters who even expect to be punished if they fall down." To bolster their confidence, he tries to show that grownups can be just as much at fault as kids, that all human beings commit *bêtises*, from time to time. *Bêtise* is a word French children are all too familiar with. "*Tu fait une bêtise,*" "You do a stupid, naughty thing," is a frequent scolding. On Izard's shows the adults can do such things, too.

He also tries to upset the image that the good guys and gals are handsome and the bad ones are ugly. "Not all children can be beautiful," he comments. "Not being beautiful doesn't mean being bad." He makes some of his villains physically attractive and some of his heroes and heroines physically unattractive. One of his big successes stars Casimir, a great frog who does many great deeds. He's just about the ugliest creature anyone has ever laid eyes on.

Izard insists that those who help him produce *Les Visiteurs* must have had enough experience with children to understand their needs. "Above all," he says, "they must *love* children."

He claims that French television producers are just beginning to understand the importance of TV for children and how it can help them. Children's TV is relatively new in France, and there aren't a great many programs. But the quality of what there is is tops.

No commercials are allowed on children's programs. They are allowed on those for adults, at the beginning and end only. Companies cannot sponsor or supervise shows. All they can do is choose the time when they would like to have their advertising appear. This is French law.

Most people see their shows in black and white, because there isn't yet a great deal of color TV in France. They can choose among telecasts offered by three national channels, operated by the government. No independent or local channels exist.

Movies in theaters are of course in color, but most young people don't see a great many of these. There are dozens of theaters in Paris and a fair number in other big cities. City children may

Winter Specials 51

see a movie a month, or more, but small and medium-size towns may have no theaters at all. For town and country boys and girls, movies are a rare treat.

Their favorites are films imported from America, especially westerns. Sometimes the sound is in English, with the French translation printed at the bottom of the screen. Sometimes French movie makers hire actors to speak the English words in French. Their voices are recorded and used instead of the American sound track. This is the same process used in TV films from America. The French call it *doublage*. If the doublage isn't expert, it gives children the giggles. They quickly detect that the actors' lip movements don't fit the words.

Many of the books young people like best to read are also translated imports from the United States. Winter is a time when they read more than during the rest of the year. The weather is the reason. In the mountains the snow piles deep, the wind whips mightily, and the cold is bitter. Elsewhere the climate is apt to be raw, with more icy rain than snow. The rawness, under a gray sky, soaks into the bones. The sun seems to be hibernating. It's a good time to get lost in a good story.

The favorites of both sexes are detective stories, animal stories, adventure stories (including cowboys, of course), and bound, hardcover books of comics. These have colorful covers and attractive end pages. The artwork is well done throughout. The dialogue is well written. The pages are nice to touch; the paper is smooth and solid. There's nothing sleazy or flimsy about French comic books.

The most popular of all French comic series is *Tin-Tin*, which has also appeared in the United States. It has been translated not only into English, but into twenty-two other languages. Tin-Tin is a boy detective. With every new volume he solves another mystery. French young people snap up new editions as fast as the publisher can put them out.

Translations of *Peter Rabbit* are beloved of small children. So is the Walt Disney version of British author Rudyard Kipling's *Mowgli*, the story of a boy brought up by wolves, from *The Jungle Book*. *Winnie the Pooh*, a book about a small bear and his forest friends by another British author, A. A. Milne, is also popular with the very young.

Laetitia Guet has all these translations on her bedroom bookshelves. She also has an encyclopedia of animal life called *Le monde animal*, *The Animal World*. Encyclopedias dealing with special fields, from animals to astronomy, are well thumbed by the young French. They read the ones that deal with their favorite subjects straight through, like other books. Then they read them over again.

A best-seller in France for almost a quarter of a century has been the story of a boy and a red balloon that followed him as a dog follows his owner, to school, to church, everywhere, much to the amazement of everyone in town. *Le Ballon Rouge* was made into a movie and the current edition is illustrated with full-page photographs from the film. Both the film and a translation of the book have appeared in the United States.

Another ongoing best-seller, for teenagers, is a book called simply *Bébé*. Accompanied by the many and beautiful illustrations that are common to all French books for young people, the text tells how a baby grows inside its mother and is born into this world. *Bébé* is one of many books that give information about how the body works.

Some books aren't really books; they are folders or cards. A folder will contain an illustrated text and records on which the text is read aloud. Cards, which are for beginning readers, have text on one side and a picture on the other.

All young people can easily get books. Besides libraries, of which there are thirty-eight thousand five hundred across the country, every town has at least one bookstore, and many have several. In cities, bookstores abound, only a few minutes' walk apart. Some devote themselves exclusively to children's books. The most famous of these is the Librarie Chantelivre in Paris. It's the size of a small library. *Librarie*, incidentally, means bookstore, not library. A library in French is a *bibliothèque*.

A traveling library, called a *bibliobus*, visits country villages. It brings all the latest editions. Residents can borrow from it on one visit and return or renew the loan on the next. The arrival of the bibliobus is eagerly awaited. The driver is sure to show up, defying, if necessary, the deepest drifts of winter.

The *muséobus* receives an equally hearty welcome. It brings museum exhibits, usually centered around a period of history, such as life in ancient Egypt. A sound track, which the driver plugs into a portable generator, explains what the exhibit is all about. Another kind of traveling display can be borrowed by schools. The bus leaves it on one trip, picks it up on the next. Students get to handle in class such objects as a caveman's stone tool or a piece of parchment on which some monk of the Middle Ages has hand-printed a prayer.

Or a class may take a trip to a museum. School classes go on a great many trips, whether to museums, ancient chateaux, or modern dams. The trip may be just for the day or may require several days. In any case, it's serious business. Before leaving, students are given a set of questions. They must find the answers from their own observations. When they return, they must supply the answers in class.

Watch this class from the collège of the town of Saint Lunéac in Brittany. The children have come to the Breton town of Pontivy, where a wing of an old chateau has been given over to an exhibit showing the region's part in the French Revolution of 1789. The students move about the display in twos and threes; partners have teamed up to find answers to certain questions. They busily write descriptions of weapons and uniforms in their notebooks. They carefully copy old maps and documents.

The big museums of Paris go out of their way to make special arrangements for school children. One even provides them with a museum of their own. Sheltered under the roof of the Musée d'Art Moderne is the Musée des Enfants. Among other exhibits is a popular model village, complete with potters, artists, and weavers at work. The processes they use are explained, and young visitors are invited to sit down and help the masters.

They also take part in some of the activities planned for them in the Georges Pompidou Center. The jam- and jelly-making demonstration is naturally a favorite—especially the tasting!

One of the trips Monsieur Soulié's class takes is to inspect the dams that control the Durance River and the hydroelectric plant that uses the dammed-up power of the river to provide electric current for the entire region. On the way, Monsieur Soulié, at the front of the bus with a microphone in hand, points out historic landmarks. Between his lectures, his pupils sing.

They sing one song in English, the black spiritual *Steal Away to Jesus*. Next they choose a haunting modern French melody: *Vous souvenez-vous?* It mourns a summer love affair that died in autumn. As they finish, they turn toward one girl, black-haired, with an orange scarf about her throat. They clap, stamp, and call her name, Mireille. Monsieur Soulié knows what they want. He holds the mike out to her. She comes to the front of the bus and repeats the song in a throaty contralto. Then she starts the group on a folksong that many students of French in the United States also know. It begins:

> *Alouette, gentille alouette,*
> *Alouette, je te plumerai,*
> *À la bec, à la tête,*
> *À la bec, à la tête,*
> *Alouette, je te plumerai.*

Lark, pretty lark, I'm going to pluck you, in the beak, in the head, in the beak, in the head, I am going to pluck you.

The song continues to pick out parts of the lark to be plucked. Meanwhile one of the girls snatches a green cap from the head of one of the boys, Bernard. His cap is tossed around the bus like a ball. When Mireille sits down, Bernard twists off her orange scarf and replaces his cap by winding the scarf about his head like a burnoose. "I am an Arab sheik," he declares. "Perhaps I will buy this hydroelectric plant." The children break up with laughter in which their prof joins.

At about eleven o'clock, silence descends on the bus. One youngster punctures it with a wail: *"Je rêve de bon jambon."* "I dream of good ham." *"Moi aussi,"* sighs another. "Me too." They are all hungry. Their parents have given them money to buy picnic provisions en route. But unless they reach some town by noon, all grocery stores will be closed for the sacred lunch hours.

At five of twelve the bus rolls into a small town. The boys and girls almost fly from the bus to a grocery store, which they spot on a corner. Two or three customers are still in the store. They have completed their purchases and Madame *la propriétaire* is about to lower the window curtains. All twenty-five students whirr past her and the customers like a flock of dive-bombing birds. As they pass they hurriedly murmur, *"Si-dames,"* a short-cut for "Messieurs, Mesdames." That's the polite greeting when one enters a store or public place where others may be gathered.

Wide-eyed, Madame and her customers acknowledge the greeting. The youngsters are now filling their net bags from the shelves. What is going on? The prof, having followed his students at a somewhat more leisurely pace, explains to Madame that they have money and wish to buy luncheon provisions. They are on a school trip. The bus, he apologizes, only just reached town. Madame is all smiles. "Les pauvres," she says. "The poor things." "Mais bien sûr, il faut absolument qu'ils mangent." "They certainly must eat." "Voila, mes enfants, j'ai du bon jambon, du fromage . . ." "See, my children, I have good ham, cheese." She does a brisk business.

Just outside the town some broad meadows with little clumps of pine offer an attractive picnic spot. At last! The youngsters choose a clump and sit in a circle. They exchange food with each other. Everybody tastes everybody else's. Then on to the power plant and the dams.

The students crawl all over the dams, measuring, photographing. Bernard decides to photograph Mireille. She poses at the lip of the dam, profiled against the sky. "Hey," says the prof, "take the dam, not her."

"I'm taking both," protests Bernard.

He, Mireille, and the others paid the equivalent in francs of sixty cents each for the trip. The school paid the rest of the cost. The students could choose whether to go or not. The trip was taken on a Wednesday. If a trip takes place during school hours and the school insists that students go, then, like the Saint Lunéac students on the trip to the chateau display, they pay only for their food. But few students ever turn down any trips. Combining comradeship with discovery, they are the young people's favorite way of learning.

Perhaps the most prized of all goals for school travel is Versailles. This palace was built by Louis XIV, whose brilliant times the Strasbourg Scouts dramatized. Versailles is just outside Paris. Depending on where a school is located, several days may have to be spent on the road, plus a full day or even two days at Versailles itself.

The reason for the attraction of the Versailles trip is the place that the palace occupies in French history. Louis, called the Sun King because of the glory with which he surrounded himself, and the many artists and writers whom he encouraged, is a source of national pride. Moreover, his palace has been the scene of important events for three centuries. Three peace treaties were signed there, the most momentous being the one that ended World War I in 1919.

The wars of modern times, as well as the French Revolution, which the Saint Lunéac students were investigating, severely damaged the palace. An American, John D. Rockefeller, Jr., gave the money to restore it. As students enter the palace, they may notice a plaque acknowledging the French people's gratitude to him.

In deep winter comes the most popular trip of all: the ski fortnight. Really more of a stay than a trip, for some schools it may last as long as three weeks. Children stay in government-financed dormitories, up to ten in each long room. Mornings, they follow their regular courses of study, with some additions related to their new environment, such as keeping temperature charts. Afternoons, they ski.

Beginners are taught how to begin. They practice on gentle slopes. Advanced skiers are taught to tackle difficult trails, jumping from heights and swerving around trees. For all, riding up on the lifts is great fun. Tiny chairs swing and sway along their cable, high above the snow-whitened mountainsides. The air is thin at this height. Cloud crystals, evaporated by the sun, quiver like chandeliers made of teardrops. The children ride through a shining mist.

Sometimes the cable grinds to a halt before the chairs have reached the top. The children don't worry. They call blithely back and forth to one another. When the cable moves again they shout "Vivat!" "Hurrah!"

Evenings are magical, say young people who have experienced them. There's a *veillée*, every night. A veillée is an evening of merrymaking. For the young skiers merrymaking means singing, storytelling, dancing, playing games, and snacking. The flame light in the huge stone fireplace flickers shadows into the corners of the dorm's big main room. Eyelids begin to droop. After an active day and an evening of fun, the young people are ready for bed.

Le ski is a passion with the French, from tots to grandparents. Almost half the population of fifty-two million ski. And most of them prefer to ski in the Alps. The French government realized that this preference for Alpine skiing could be turned into a moneymaker for a region that desperately needed money. Today, through an agency that helps different regions develop their special resources, it pays part of the cost of building ski lodges. The government also pays part of the bill for renting rooms in a lodge. In some a family can stay for what would amount to only $2 per day per person in American money. And for the children, ski lessons are free.

The popularity of Alpine skiing, plus government help in bringing down its cost, has made a world of difference in the lives of Alpine families. Once winter cut villagers off not only from the rest of the country, but even from the next village. Now that roads are open for skiers, students can get to school. They can meet, mix, and mingle with youngsters from all France. Rickety homes have been repaired. Sheep and cattle that were bony because of poor feed are now plump. Food on the table is hearty and clothing on the back is warm. There was always fun to be had in the winter snow but now there is comfort besides.

ANOTHER WINTER INTERLUDE that every youngster looks forward to is Noël, Christmas. The holiday is celebrated differently in different families and different regions, but some parts of the celebration are the same everywhere. Most families go to church, either at midnight on Christmas Eve, or else on Christmas morning. Mountain people tend to prefer the morning service. Midnight in the mountains can be bitter cold in winter.

Christmas dinner, always big, is eaten either on Christmas Eve or on Christmas day. Parents, children, grandparents, cousins, uncles, aunts all gather around the table. In the country home of Monsieur and Madame Bonnaud near the little village of Nant d'Aveyron some fifty miles northwest of Montpellier, forty-four people in all celebrate the holiday together. Fourteen grandchildren and their parents keep Christmas with their grandparents.

The children sleep in a dormitory, which the Bonnaud's have built especially for them. On the door of the dining room hangs something that resembles a beautifully embroidered shoe bag. But the pockets hold napkins instead of shoes. Above each pocket, Grandma Bonnaud has embroidered the name of a grandchild. After meals, children return their folded napkins to their own slots.

At the home of Antoine and Dominique de Champeaux twenty relatives sit down to dinner on Christmas eve. Champagne is served. On this holiday young people everywhere are allowed a glassful. A few days earlier, the boys went to the forest with their father to help cut the Christmas tree. Together they hauled it home. People who live near forests cut their own trees. Others have to buy them. Along with the tree, a *bûche* is brought or bought. A bûche is a small log, hollowed out and filled with pine or holly. Sometimes there are chocolate bûches for children to eat.

In almost every household the crèche, the manger scene at the birth of Christ, is set up in a place of honor. In the Bonnaud family, the scene is spread out on the dining room sideboard. The fourteen grandchildren cut pine boughs to surround it.

The figures around a family's manger may have been carved by a great grandparent or even a great-great-grandparent. Many have been handed down for generations. In Provence, especially, the manger scene includes not only the familiar figures of the baby Jesus, Mary, Joseph, shepherds, and wisemen, but ordinary people as well. Fishermen with their rods, women toting jugs of water or bundles of twigs for broom-making, a hunter with his gun, farmers carrying rakes over their shoulders, millers lugging bags of flour, bakers with loaves of bread under their arms—all these form part of the procession heading toward the manger.

These figures are called *santons*. Their name comes from a word in Provençal dialect, *santoun*, which means little saint. The parade of santons toward the crèche reflects Christmas in Provence seven or eight hundred years ago, when lords and ladies invited the village folk to share Christmas with them in their castle. These days, the santons have become so well liked that their appearance at the manger is no longer limited to Provence. The Bonnauds have some in their crèche.

Presents, of course, are part of Christmas everywhere. French people may receive theirs on Christmas eve or Christmas day or both. Antoine and Dominique exchange gifts with their parents on Christmas morning. On Christmas Eve they exchange them with the other relatives. The Bonnaud grandchildren and their parents already have their presents from each other before setting out for the country home at Nant d'Aveyron. On Christmas morning comes the second round with the grandparents. Very small children may receive additional presents from *Père Noël*, Father Christmas. He's the French Santa Claus.

Throughout the land, Christmas renews these traditional customs, along with fulfilling traditions special to certain regions. For example, everybody eats Christmas dinner, but what people eat varies widely. Turkey is a favorite, but the Bonnaud children prefer goose. Eric Belledent likes rabbit. Breton children choose fish. In Corsica the main dish may be either a baby goat or a leg of lamb. Goat is popular in the Vosges mountains, too, as is duck.

Laetitia Guet usually has guinea hen, but the real dinner of Provence is cod. It's served with cauliflower and a spinach omelet, boiled thistle stalks in a white sauce, celery, and snails. There are seven wines and thirteen desserts!

Since each dish is of course eaten separately, the Christmas meal may last almost five hours. Before sitting down, father pours sweet wine over the bûche, saying:

> À l'an qui ven!
> E, si sian pas mai, siegen pas me!

The words, in old Provençal dialect, a mixture of French, Spanish, and Italian, mean: "To the year that is coming! And if we are not more, let us not be fewer!"

Outside, the voices of carolers may be heard, accompanying themselves with flutes and tambourines. Some of them may have donned costumes such as the santons wear. Christmas is a very gay time in Provence, a time that begins on December fourth with a household ceremony. Children place grains of wheat or lentil seeds on a small plate covered with a damp cloth. They dampen the cloth as often as needed to keep it moist. As Christmas nears, they inspect the plate anxiously. Are the seeds or grains beginning to sprout? Everyone hopes they will do so by Christmas, when they are to be placed in front of the crèche. Sprouting seeds mean a happy year ahead for the family.

December fourth is also the opening of the Christmas season in the Vosges mountains of Alsace. On that day Saint Nicholas drives his cart through villages such as Colroy-La-Roche, stopping at schools like the two-roomer there. The original Saint Nicholas was a fourth century bishop, so the Alsatian Christmas saint wears a bishop's pointed mitre on his head and long flowing robes. With him travels the *fouettard*, the whipper, dressed all in black and carrying his snaky whip.

Saint Nicholas gives candies to children who have behaved well during the year. The fouettard scolds and cracks his whip at children who have not. The two men who act these parts have been chosen by community officials in each area. Parents and teachers have supplied them with information that allows them to sort out which children to reward.

In some communities the saint travels without the fouettard. The whip-cracker has been known to frighten small children badly. Some have even skipped school on December fourth rather than face him. Officials decided this wouldn't do. They outlawed the fouettard.

In Strasbourg, Christmas transforms the city. The Rue des Halberds—Halberd Street—becomes a children's ski slope. The street takes its name from the halberds—axlike medieval weapons—affixed at regular intervals to the second stories of buildings. This is Strasbourg's smart shopping mall.

Down the center, from December 4th on, run tracks. On these youngsters can be transported by electric skis. Above them the halberds sprout pine boughs. Alongside the tracks are mock chalets. The tracks run over mock mountains. Little ones in the Rotterdam Scout troop of Strasbourg look forward to this ride every

Winter Specials

Christmas. Rose Pascal and the other scouts like to visit the crèche in the Orangerie. It's alive! Actual people, standing still as still, make up the manger scene.

Christmas merrymaking isn't at an end by December twenty-sixth. On New Year's Day there may be more gift giving. The holiday of the Three Kings comes on January sixth. In Provence, on that day, cakes made in the shape of kings are served. In one cake there's a bean. Whoever finds it is king or queen for the day and chooses a queen or king to help reign in the family. The crèche, the log, and the tree may remain until the second of February. That's the official end of the season. By then, spring and other holidays are only a couple of months away.

Breton schoolchildren at goûté during a class trip.

Above: Monsieur Soulié's class on their trip to the Durance River dams. AUTHOR'S PHOTO

Right: Students at a ski fortnight. FRENCH CULTURAL SERVICES

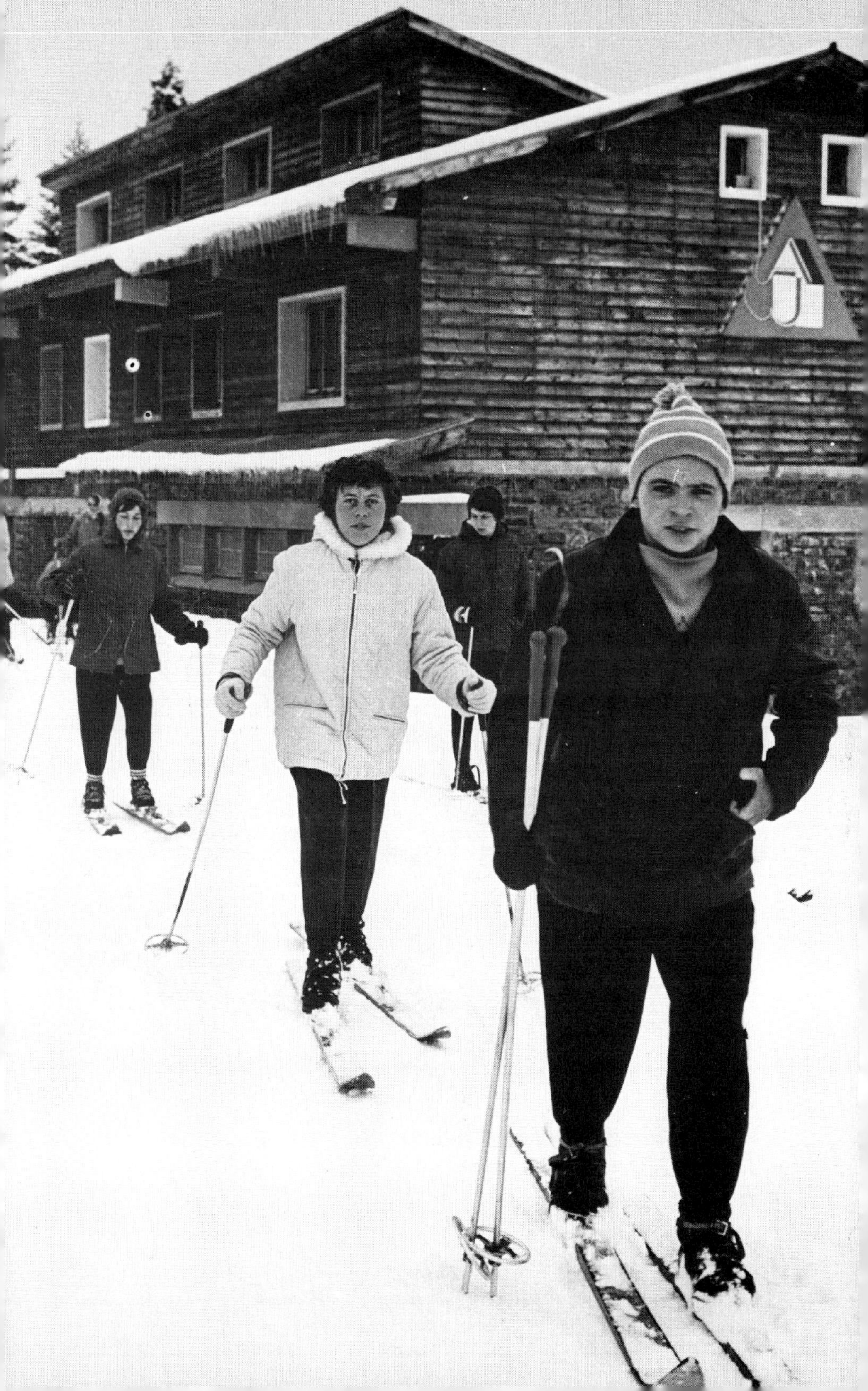

The family napkin holder made and embroidered by Grandmother Bonnaud.

Some of the Bonnaud grandchildren.

Above: Santons for the Christmas manger scene. FRENCH CULTURAL SERVICES

Right: A Provençal Christmas ceremony —Offering the Lamb. FRENCH CULTURAL SERVICES

5
Returning Light

IN SPRING the rain loses its iciness. Snow ceases, except in the mountains. Everyone is impatient for the return of long, sunny days. But the sun seems in no hurry. Spring rains can be heavy. They are what makes the land so green in summer, the crops so tender and abundant. In dry springs, crops wither on parched land. Farmers suffer and food prices rise.

People understand the necessity for the days-at-a-time deluges of spring; still they can't help hoping the rain will soon be over. Mountain youngsters, especially, hope for a sunny spring. This is the time of year when their schools send them down to the seashore and river valleys for two weeks of combined schoolwork and sports. Who wants to go to the beach or run a race on a rainy day?

In Provence, *boule* teams keep hopeful eyes on the heavens. The Provençaux are great boule fans. They play the game with iron balls, a little smaller than bowling balls, but much, much heavier. Usually the players set up in a town square or open courtyard. A small ball is placed at the far end. Each player tries to hit it with his big one. He also tries to hit the balls of the opposite team in such a way as to knock them out of position and, if possible, take that position for himself.

The balls are much too heavy for a child to sling, but by the time boys reach twelve many start to practice in out-of-the-way alleys and nooks. Boule players are big in their gallery of heroes. They set their sights on becoming as skilled as their village victors.

Children who are looking forward to Carnival also hope for sunny days. Carnival comes in chancy weather, forty days before Easter. Nowhere is this celebration more colorful than in Alsace. Alsatian children don comical masks, oversize shoes, and big hats. They shuffle along in bands, begging candies from door to door. In some Vosges Mountain villages, girls masquerade as fairies and witches, boys as elves and demons. The fairies and elves battle the witches and demons. The battle always ends in victory for the fairies and elves. Their victory symbolizes the triumph of spring over winter.

This pageant was inherited from German neighbors across the River Rhine. Germany and France are only a hop, skip, and jump apart in northern Alsace. In modern times, Alsace has twice changed hands between the two countries. In the early history of Europe, tribes and monarchs on both sides of the Rhine fought again and again for possession of the territory.

The next celebration in which youngsters play a large part is Le Rêve de Pentecôte, the dream of Pentecost, as the French call this holiday, which comes after Easter. It honors the descent of the Holy Spirit to the disciples of Christ. Pentecost is a country-wide occasion for daylong parades. Many of the floats are conceived and manned by young people—in the Provencal village of Apt, almost exclusively so.

Hours before the parade starts, onlookers line the streets. They chat with policemen in full dress; blue coats with scarlet-lined coattails, shining black boots, spanking white gloves with deep, flaring cuffs. Finally the floats start to roll. Between them, boys and girls half march, half dance to the spirited music of youth bands. The crowd gasps, then cheers as a teenage majorette in a silver-spangled turquoise costume tosses two batons fifty feet in the air, turns a handspring, and catches the batons in descent. She repeats her act every thirty yards. She's likely to win a prize. On Pentecost night, the best floats and most accomplished performers receive awards from the town officials.

A GREAT MANY VILLAGES have their own special celebrations in honor of their own special saints. Not far from Apt, in the tiny village of Monteux, certain boys look forward every May sixteenth to the evening church bells, which announce the Fête of Saint Gens. Gens was an early twelfth century hermit. He is supposed to have withdrawn to a rocky fastness in the area, dying there on May sixteenth, when he was twenty-two. His prayers, meanwhile, were credited with producing miracle crops.

On the date of his death every year, four teenage boys wearing yellow turbans take turns, two by two, carrying an image of the saint to a hermitage named for him. The boys are chosen by the vote of village citizens. They are preceded by a fifth, younger boy, carrying a rose-garlanded cross. Behind them comes a horse-drawn carriage full of Monteux dignitaries. The horses sport yellow cockades on their foreheads. Yellow ribbons are braided into their manes.

The boys often break into a jog. Nevertheless, they take nearly four hours to cover the nine miles between Monteux and the hermitage, because every cluster of houses along the way has set up a welcome for them with fireworks and refreshments. The procession grows longer and longer as more and more people join it, some on foot, some in autos or farm trucks—the latter full of children.

About ten o'clock at night the crowd arrives at the hermitage. Others, who have journeyed from all Provence, are already there. A service is held, entirely in the old dialect of the region. Enriched by many voices, hymns roll out into the night in magnificent harmony. At the end of the service the congregation draws a deep breath and lets it out in a thundering olé!

Afterward comes a tremendous feast. Those who have taken part in the procession troop to a nearby house where the women of Monteux have loaded long tables. Bernard Brès, a boy who helped the priest at the altar during the service, looks at the high-piled platters with eyes like saucers. At the sight of the food, he forgets how tired he is from the long walk and the late hours. Bernard Brès is the son of a Monteux fruit and tomato farmer. The current ambition of his life is to be chosen to carry the cross in this festival. His mouth full, he looks with envy at this year's crucifer, the cross-carrier, seated between the priest and the mayor. One of the women pats him on the shoulder and whispers, "I heard a rumor, Bernard, that you were to be chosen, next year." Bernard's envy changes to hope.

ANOTHER UNIQUE FESTIVAL is the Fête de Dieu in northern Brittany, which takes place the first Sunday after Pentecost. Supposedly, Jesus is about to visit the region. The fête springs from an old legend that claims that Jesus's mother, Mary, was a Breton. When her son died, she returned from the Holy Land to her home. After his resurrection, Jesus came to visit her there.

The holiday is celebrated with parades along flower-decorated streets. Similar parades are held in honor of various saints all summer long in Brittany. They are called Pardons, because the marchers ask forgiveness for their sins.

All those who take part, children and adults alike, dress up in costumes of long ago. These costumes, richly embroidered and ornamented with velvet bands, may be handed down in families for several generations. Between special occasions, such as a Pardon or a wedding, they are carefully wrapped and hung away in closets. The styles differ from section to section of Brittany. Each has favorites.

Perhaps the most interesting part of the costume is the headgear of women and girls. These are high caps, decorated with lace or made entirely of lace. They come in four different shapes. Especially beguiling is a fashion from the town of Pont L'Abbé, in the southwest corner of Brittany. A column of stiffened lace a foot and a half high is perched on the middle of the head, with broad lace streamers flying down the back. Many of the women and girls of the area are too pleased with their lace columns to save them for special occasions. They show them off every day.

The costumed marchers in a Pardon usually chant as they walk. They carry banners with crosses and pictures of saints. Saints' statues are carried by teenage girls. After the parade there are sports contests and dancing to the music of bagpipes and bassoons.

One of the contests is a kind of wrestling match performed only in Brittany. Two young men, wearing shorts and billowing blouses with a sash at the waist, open the match by kissing each other three times. Then they grab each other by the neck, each using his feet to try to trip his opponent and cast him to the ground.

RELIGIOUS FESTIVALS, filled with gaiety, delight not just church people but everybody. Actually, practicing church members aren't numerous and neither is the assortment of faiths. About two percent of the French are Jewish and another two percent Protestant. Unlike Protestants elsewhere, French Protestants aren't divided into different churches. They are all one: *The* French Protestant Church.

Foreign nations have established a few other churches for their citizens in France. The Americans have an Episcopal Church, for example, and the British an Anglican one. There's a group of Quakers and clusters of Moslems. Ninety percent of the French say their religion is Roman Catholic. But only twenty percent of these claim to attend church regularly. It's the same with the Protestants.

Northerners tend to go more faithfully than southerners. When Tante Nicole travels from Paris to visit the Guets in Provence, she always worships on Sundays, but she can't persuade them to come with her. Of course, there are exceptions to this north-south rule. Laetitia Guet's girl friend, Véronique, and the Bonnaud grandchildren never miss a Sunday service unless they're sick. Some northerners go only at Christmas. The magic of that candle-lit service with carols touches everyone. Everywhere regulars and irregulars pack churches.

For the Bonnaud grandchildren, a highlight of their early church activities is their first communion. As is the Catholic custom, that service is followed by a party for the child who has received the communion wafer for the first time. Every member of the family is invited, from the youngest to the oldest, including all cousins, uncles, and aunts. Each brings a present for the new communicant. It's like Christmas, only more so.

Besides the Bible and crucifix from parents, the closest relatives usually give money. Remembering how much she received, granddaughter Celline says, "I got one hundred francs" (an amount close to twenty dollars). "I got two hundred," recalls her cousin Pascal. Little cousins Béatrice and Jean-Paul can hardly wait until they are old enough for their communions, and that's a fact. Jean-Paul has already decided what he will buy with his gift money: gadgets for his bike. "Some should be saved for *l'offrande*," Béatrice says. L'offrande is the offering in church.

Another happy religious holiday is observed by French Protestants. In the sixteenth and seventeenth centuries, Catholics burned Protestant houses of worship and killed many worshipers in bloody wars. Survivors fled the country.

When the wars were over, survivors returned. Churches were rebuilt, congregations reunited. Today, Protestants celebrate this reunion annually. The date of the celebration differs from place to place, depending on the date of the local revival. Often the festival lasts several days. It's not unusual for families from all over, in and out of France, to make a pilgrimage to the church of their great-great, or even great-great-great, grandparents. In and around the site, cars are parked bumper to bumper. Every home is filled to the roof with relatives from near and far.

After morning services, the town takes on the air of a country fair. Children ride up, down, and round and round on the merry-go-round, or drive toy autos over dizzily twisting tracks, shrieking lustily. The aroma of mouthwatering merguès floats in spits of smoke from a booth where these hot, spiced sausages are being grilled. The tempting sizzle of batter poured into bubbling butter halts passers-by at the crêpe stand. Children debate: do they want theirs stuffed with ham, cheese, fish, or jam? On this day they are quick to take advantage of their parents' generous mood.

The rest of the year in a Protestant home children know little of the spirit the French call *joie de vivre*, the sheer joy of living each day. Feelings are not to be displayed in public. When visiting, or receiving guests, the family keeps within a circle of like-minded Protestant friends. And as young Protestants grow up, they are strictly forbidden to marry outside their faith.

Small, sober, and close-knit, this group nevertheless has an influence much bigger than one might expect. Many of them are leaders in businesses that control the flow of money. Others are among the top men in industries that employ more than half the workers of France.

They do much to help the old, the sick, the poor, the jobless, all people in need. They try to see that everyone has a chance to enjoy the good things in France.

Especially they work for children. They train the handicapped, rescue juvenile delinquents, and offer vacation opportunities. They push for the new ways that are gradually taking over in schools.

EVEN IN THE MOST MODERN OF SCHOOLS, and never mind how much some pupils may enjoy their classes, all are glad when school lets out for summer. The first day of summer, June 21st, falls on the date of the festival of Saint John. In the countryside around Strasbourg bonfires are lighted at night to celebrate both. They are carefully tended to make certain they won't spread. Sometimes boys and girls jump over small fires, as though jumping rope. The saying goes that if a boy and girl jump over a fire together, they will grow up to marry each other. Like the carnival pageant in this same area, the fire jumping has German roots.

About three weeks after Saint John's Day comes the biggest holiday of the summer, indeed the most historic holiday in all the year. That's Bastille Day, July 14th. On that date in 1789, citizens of Paris stormed an ancient prison, the Bastille, into which prisoners were thrown without trial, just on the say-so of the monarch. The attack opened the French Revolution, which was the beginning of France's change from a monarchy to a republic.

The longest parade marches down the widest avenue in the world—the Champs Élysées in Paris. Champs Élysées sidewalks alone are as wide as streets in most big cities. On July 14, not only the sidewalks but the parking lanes are jammed with onlookers. Every bench on the green strips that separate the parking lanes from the avenue is taken. Small children are carried on their fathers' shoulders, so they can see over the heads of the crowd.

The Garde Republicaine, which is a sort of home guard,

usually heads the parade. Astride black horses, the guardsmen wear shining helmets crested with plumes. Their uniforms are black, white, and scarlet. Behind them may come paratroopers with black berets, the tank corps with green berets, naval cadets in crisp white. Sometimes they are joined by troops from African countries that were once colonies of France, but are now independent members of La Communauté, an international association of French-speaking nations. Some of these troops may ride camels.

Planes fly overhead. At the end, six jets zoom low. They let out streams of smoke, blue on one side of the avenue, red on the other side, and white in the middle. The blue, white, and red stripes of the French flag rest suspended in the air. The people cheer and break into their national anthem, the "Marseillaise," which was the theme song of the French Revolution.

In the afternoon, smaller parades march through all the neighborhoods of Paris. In other cities and towns the afternoon is usually given over to sports contests. At night, everywhere, there is a grand display of fireworks. Above all France, the sky explodes with rockets that make myriad designs: fish, fountains, flowers.

Nor is the day yet finished. When the fireworks cease, street dancing begins. On this night of nights, children are allowed to stay up till all hours. They dance with their friends to the music of small orchestras hired by cafe owners. Strings of colored lights have been strung across the sidewalks in front of the cafes. Between dances, children and parents rest at small outdoor tables, sipping coffee or cold drinks and munching sandwiches.

A mere seventeen days later comes a long-awaited event: family vacation. Discussions of where to go started in the dead of winter and grew warmer as returning light warmed the earth. On the first day of August these discussions bear fruit. August is the month almost everyone takes off. Traffic is dead in the cities. Store curtains are lowered, homes shuttered. Large industries close for the entire month. All activity is transferred to the mountains or the seashore or wherever in the country families have chosen to go. Rural France is invaded, swamped by vacationers. The beaches of the Atlantic and the Mediterranean are draped with people. Campers' tents, multicolored, coat the mountainsides and line the banks of valley streams. A frequent answer to the annual where-shall-we-go-this-year question is, let's visit the grandparents. The Bonnaud children take turns every summer in Grandma's and Grandpa's country home.

Lucky the child whose grandparents live in Brittany. It's a top favorite vacation spot for the French. The days of swimming, boating, exploring seem to fly by. Wandering through the shoulder-high ferns that feather Breton bluffs, children gather primroses. They hunt for mussels in the tide-strewn seaweed on Breton beaches. Mother steams these in white wine with garlic or shallots, butter, lemon juice, and many fresh herbs. No one will leave any of the sauce on his plate. Every drop will be soaked up with a piece of bread.

Other children vacation at a *colonie de vacances*. The colonies or *centres* (centers) were founded by the Protestant Church, later taken over by the government. They are sponsored by the Secretariat for Youth and Sports. Laetitia Guet enrolls in one that specializes in the teaching of music. Eric Belledent attends one at which children learn construction skills by repairing or helping put up buildings needed in neighboring communities.

There are thirteen thousand of these centers throughout France. They are used every year by some one and a half million youngsters between the ages of four and eighteen. The young people combine work with play. Some engage in projects to protect the environment. Others make movies or produce pottery. An enormous variety of opportunities is offered. And after the workday comes the veillée for which the centers are noted. Ask any child who's enjoyed one.

Families also travel outside France during vacation, usually in Spain or Portugal, because costs are low in these countries. In or out of France, a big problem with vacation travel is what to do with the pets. There's a dog in most families in France, and often a cat or two as well. Not to mention the hamsters, guinea pigs, rabbits, turtles, canaries, parrots, magpies, and doves. Wherever possible, pets travel with the family. Dogs almost always do. Dogs are allowed in the rooms of many hotels. They can even accompany their owners to a good number of restaurants.

AT HARVEST TIME there is more merrymaking. In all the wine regions of France, people again dance in the streets. They may also parade. In the Jura mountains, south of the Vosges, women and children tie hundreds of bunches of grapes together to form one huge bunch, so heavy that four men are needed to carry it. These four lead the parade, followed by vineyard workers carrying halberds decorated with grape leaves. To the tune of violins, the parade marches to the local church, where the enormous bunch is hung from the ceiling. After the service the dancing begins.

In Auvergne, the dance is the *bourrée*. The bourrée tells a story about a young man pursuing the girl he wants to marry. He catches up with her, but she refuses him. He turns away, but she relents and recalls him.

Agricultural fairs are as numerous as wine festivals in Auvergne. They are the setting for much bargaining and many bourrées. Eric Belledent has been to several with his father, who brings cattle there to sell. When he and a customer agree on price, the two shake hands, order drinks from a stall, and clink glasses. The handshake and the clinking seal the agreement.

Eric likes the bourrée, but he likes rock even better. The interests of French children span time. Dominique de Champeaux sails his raft, but he is envious of Antoine's motorbike. The family hears the whir of their dishwasher between their after-dinner folk songs. Laetitia Guet certainly enjoys her bike, but she gladly gives up cycling when she has a chance to ride her father's shiny new tractor.

Young people's passion for hiking on their own two feet en plein air—in the open air—isn't cooled off by being crowded into a tiny car with brothers, sisters, pets, and luggage, and whizzing on four- to six-lane highways to reach a chosen vacation spot. They clamor for a gouté, a midafternoon snack, at one of the McDonald's Hamburger or Kentucky Fried Chicken stands or pizza palaces en route. They wash it down with Coca-Cola, everywhere available, even at the little out-of-the-way Ardèche beach where Laetitia swims. Still, the fast food doesn't at all affect their appetite for their mothers' fine French cooking. They are growing up in a modern country that honors old traditions. So they can gouter with Coke and carry the cross for Saint Gens.

But, as vacation time draws to a close, the young French have something else on their minds. Once more the rentrée is coming. Reluctantly like Laetitia and Dominique, or gladly like Eric Belledent, they begin to assemble their clothes, their rainbow-colored pen and pencil cases, their notebooks with pages ruled off in small squares.

They will meet old friends in their classrooms and make new ones. Some will have Spanish, Italian, or German sounding names. They will all speak French, but they may speak it differently. In many schools, as in much of their country, there is refreshing variety. So come, rentrée. Even if lessons are boring, there are sure to be boys and girls who are not!

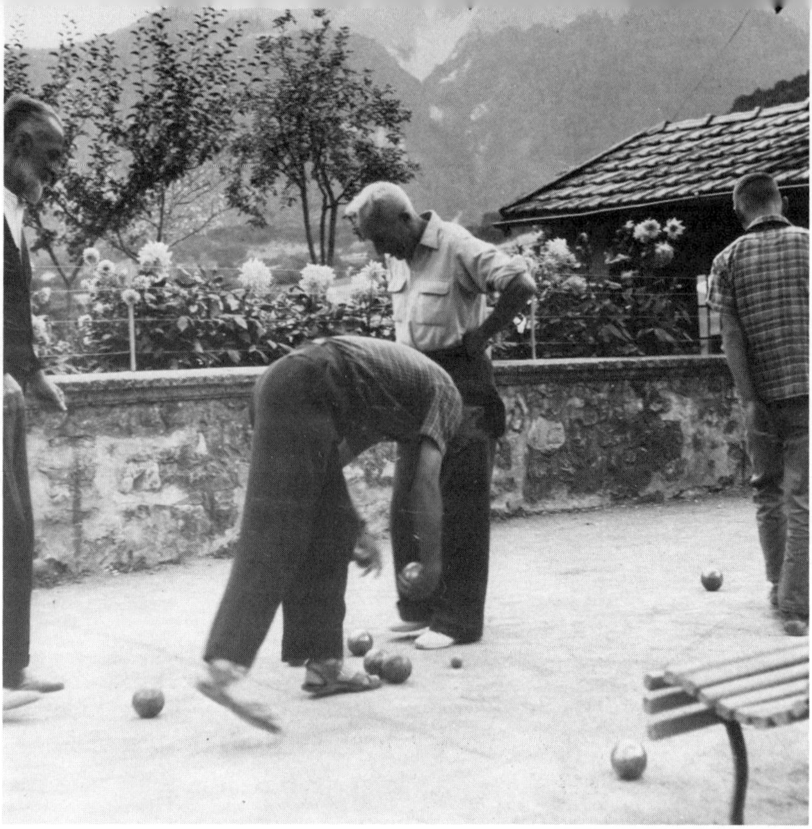

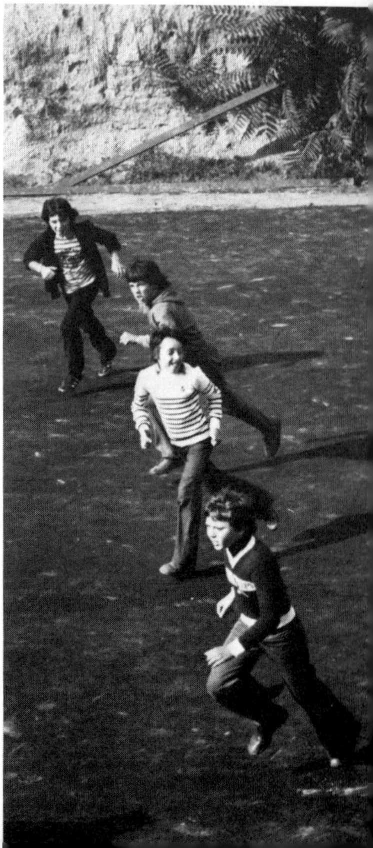

Left: Men playing boule in Provence. FRENCH CULTURAL SERVICES

Below: Students on Corsica, as well as in the rest of France, play soccer in their free time.

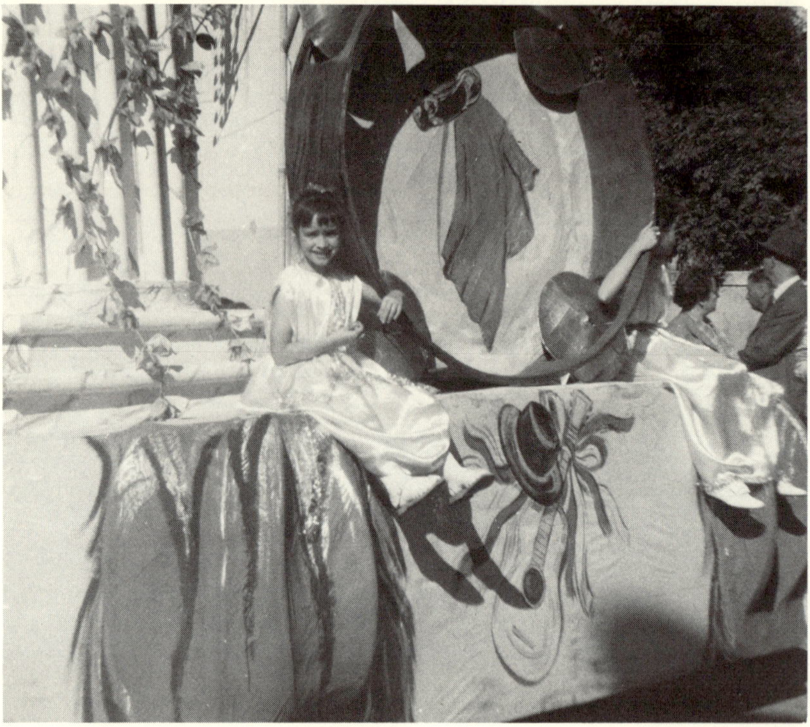

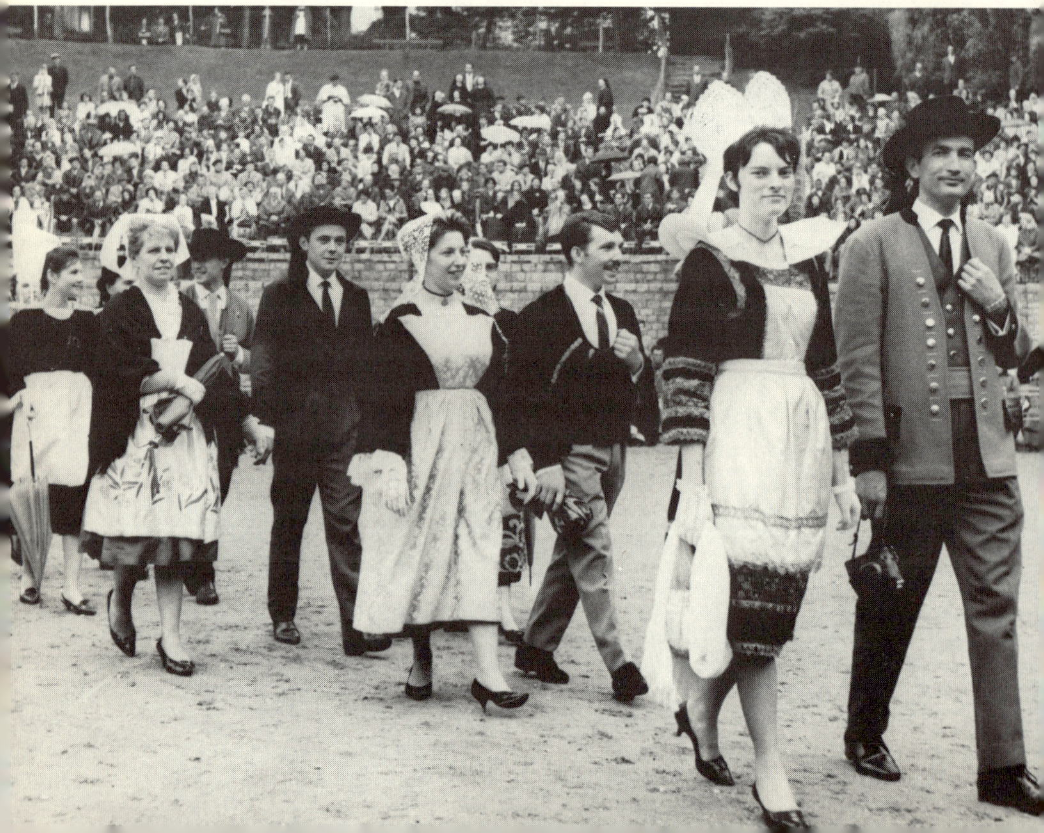

Above left: One of the floats in La Rêve de Pentecôte parade in Apt. AUTHOR'S PHOTO

Below left: Marchers in a Breton pardon. FRENCH CULTURAL SERVICES

Below: A small Breton girl shows off her ornate cap. FRENCH CULTURAL SERVICES

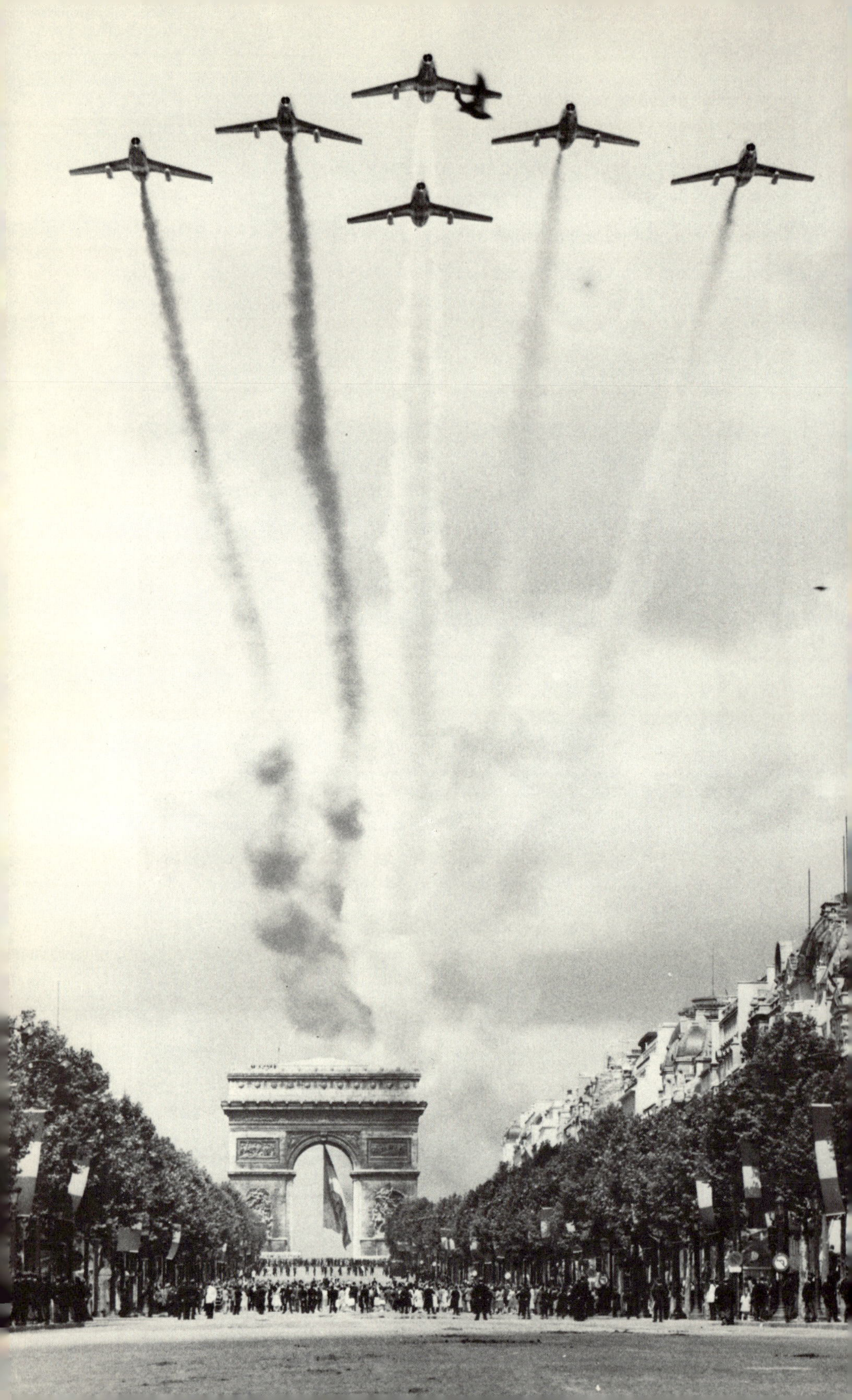

Bastille Day celebrations in Paris. FRENCH CULTURAL SERVICES

6
French With Spice

CHILDREN RETURNING TO SCHOOL in Paris and the near suburbs of the city are likely to have some classmates who have come from Algeria in North Africa. That country was once a French colony. After it gained independence in 1963, Algerians began migrating to France in search of jobs they couldn't find at home. By the end of the 1970s well over a million and a half had arrived. More still come every year. They are the largest group of foreign-born people living in France.

Fathers usually come first. As soon as they are employed they send for their families, big ones with as many as eight or nine children. The majority settle in and around Paris, because that's where the most work is. Quite a few, however, locate in the south of France, particularly in Provence, because the climate is somewhat nearer to the year-round warm weather they left behind.

Eleven-year-old Fatima Beribiche, her sisters Dsamiila, Farida, and Yamina, her brothers Aziz, Ahmed, and Youssef—all teenagers—live with their parents in a housing project in Colombes, a twenty-minute train ride from Paris. The children are a handsome lot, dark-haired, dark-eyed, with long lashes.

The Beribiche apartment, up four flights of stairs, is crowded

French With Spice   7 7

when everybody is at home. Even when they aren't, necessary furniture occupies most of the space. But the apartment has a good bathroom and a good kitchen and central heating. Certainly it's a great improvement over the Paris tenement where Mr. Beribiche roomed when he first arrived. That building had no inside plumbing and no central heating. That's the sort of housing seventy percent of new Algerian arrivals have to put up with still.

When he could finally afford to bring his family to France, Fatima was not yet born. She is the only one born in France. She knows nothing of the old ways, the old customs at home, that her parents talk so much about. Except for Youssef and Farida, the two oldest, the others don't remember a thing about the country they left, and even those two remember less and less.

Once the family returned to Algeria for a vacation. The parents didn't like the idea of their children forgetting the homeland. Air Algérie, the Algerian airline, in cooperation with the French government, makes inexpensive flights possible between the two countries. But even an inexpensive trip is expensive for most Algerian families. The Beribiche family scraped and saved to afford the fare.

Fatima, Dsamiila, Yamina, and Farida are just as well pleased that the trip costs too much to repeat. In Algeria they had to follow the old custom that kept them cooped up in the house of their relatives, so they would be sure to avoid contact with boys. Aziz, Ahmed, and Youssef, on the other hand, went to a beach every day. They enjoyed the swimming. The girls never want to go back. Never.

Not that the girls have as much freedom as they would like, even in Colombes. Their parents see to that. But school is their salvation. Eight hours a day, five days a week, while school is in session, they are out from under their parents' rules. They are in classes with boys. Teachers treat them as the equals of boys. They are given opportunities for learning that their parents think are necessary only for boys. No wonder they love school.

The no-no's for girls stem from the Moslem religion. The Moslem god is Allah, whose prophet was Mohammed. Certain of Mohammed's sayings were later interpreted to mean that girls weren't good for much, except raising children and keeping house. They were to be seen abroad as little as possible and to stay strictly away from all males except members of their family.

Algerian girls in France quickly see that other girls aren't bound by any such rules. Other girls have boyfriends. Other girls have dates. So why shouldn't they? Then the family argument begins.

Father would like to take his daughters out of school by the time they are ten. From his point of view, they have then had as much education as girls need. In Algeria, he would have married them off by that age. Fortunately, the Beribiche girls don't have to fight to stay in school. It's against the law for them to leave that young.

Even with the boys there are differences of opinion about education. Mr. Beribiche wants his sons to continue school, but he wants them trained, from an early age, for manual work. What good, he asks, are these courses in languages, literature, social studies, and art? They don't help a man earn a living.

Aziz, Ahmed, and Youssef don't see it that way. They want the same advantages as other boys in their schools. They want everything that's coming to them. Their classmates talk of becoming lawyers, doctors, engineers, earth scientists. So why not the Beribiche boys?

As for girls, they are of course supposed to have no career ambitions at all. Unless, that is, they want jobs as hairdressers, seamstresses, or any occupation that will keep them strictly in the company of women. But secretaries, sales girls, nurses, airline stewardesses—never! Nonetheless, Algerian girls are increasingly finding ways to get into the working world. When parents remain adamant, many solve the problem by running away from home. The runaway rate among teenage Algerian girls is exceedingly high.

Both boys and girls get into trouble with their parents about clothes. Mr. Beribiche doesn't approve of his sons' tight pants or his daughters' short skirts. He doesn't approve, either, of the children's jeans. He won't let his daughters wear makeup. "Not until you are married," he says. So they make up when they reach school and take off the makeup before they come home. He fumes about the records of current song hits that they borrow from friends. Too sexy. So the children play them when he's out of the apartment. He forbids them to read comic books. They contain too many drawings of the human figure. That's against Moslem rules. They keep their comic books hidden.

Language is another problem. Most Algerians speak a little French, because the language has been handed down since the days when the country was a French colony. However, older Algerians prefer to speak their native language when they are among themselves. Not so the children. They are grateful for the special cram courses in French in school. They prefer to speak the language of their French friends. When their parents address them in their native language, the Beribiche children reply in French. Mr. and Mrs. Beribiche shake their heads. They had hoped to preserve the language of the homeland in their family. The children couldn't care less. They don't live there any more.

Boys don't have quite as hard a time in the family as girls. The oldest boy is, after the father, the family boss. He can push the other kids around. Even his mother looks up to him. She was brought up to favor male children, especially the oldest male, above females. On the birthdays of Aziz, Ahmed, and Youssef she arranges big parties. For Fatima, Dsamiila, Farida, and Yamina she plans no such gala events. This makes the girls all the angrier. But Youssef, who is the oldest boy, thinks it's just as well his sisters are kept in their place.

Throughout these conflicts, Mrs. Beribiche says very little. She was brought up to obey first her parents, later her husband and husband's mother. She is baffled by the defiance in her family. Such a thing would never have happened at home. Should they have stayed there?

As for Mr. Beribiche, he sighs. "What good is it to earn a living in France, if to do so a family must lose its honor, its religion, and its children?"

To which Youssef replies, "It is I who am educating you, and not the other way around."

Between teenage Algerians and their parents the gulf is very wide. The parents are sad and bewildered. The young people are in turmoil on two fronts; at home and among the French of their age with whom they long to be friends. Their religion makes a difference between them and the French. Contrary to what their parents may think, very few have given up their religion. One of its commandments forbids eating the flesh of pigs. When pork, sausage, or ham is served at school lunch, they skip it. During a Moslem holiday, called Ramadan, which lasts for a month, they fast during the day and don't eat or drink anything at all in school. They have breakfast before sunrise and then have supper after sunset. They believe that the daylight fast keeps the devil in chains. The end of Ramadan is celebrated by three days of feasting, with lots of candy for the children.

The observance of Ramadan and the forbidding of pork are decreed in the Koran, the Moslem Bible. Few young Algerians would break these laws. It is the later additions about social behavior that make no sense to them.

French With Spice   81

The eating customs don't make sense to their French schoolmates. What French student would think of skipping a meal or refusing a succulent piece of pork? To avoid their schoolmates' stares, Algerian youngsters tend to bunch together in the school cafeteria, apart from the others. Then the others think they are being snobbish. In schools where Algerian students are numerous, they may be given special menus. The French reaction is: how come they get something different from us? The Algerian youngster can't win.

Also there's the question of age. Algerians not born in France are usually well behind their age group in studies. They have come from primitive schools. Consequently, they have to be placed in classes with students younger than they are until they catch up. The age difference is too great to offer any chance of making friends. Much as education is desired, school can be lonely.

After graduation, job seeking raises another hurdle. As a rule, Algerians are hired only when employers can't find anybody else, and they are fired before anybody else. This is particularly true for professional jobs, with a few exceptions, such as the Union of Mediterranean Banks, which has North African connections, Air Algérie, and others that do business with Algeria. In a sense, Mr. Beribiche was right when he insisted that his sons needed training for manual work. More Algerian men are employed in the building trades than in any others. Even there, the rule still holds: last hired, first fired. We need the jobs for ourselves, say French workers.

This is not the attitude of the French government. A law passed in July 1972 declares that refusal of employment on the basis of a person's national origin is illegal. Provision is made for suing an employer who disobeys the law. But where does the average Algerian get the money to hire a lawyer and sue?

Trade unions are ready to stand up for the rights of Algerian workers, the same as for all their members. But few immigrants from Algeria join unions. They are uncertain; they are afraid. They don't want to make a misstep.

The children of Algerian immigrants, among them the Beribiche youngsters, are likely to change this lie-low pattern. They feel more French than Algerian, despite differences in customs between themselves and their French comrades. Not having had to endure as much as their parents did, they are less afraid and more adventurous.

Still, as they grow into men and women they will hear people say, "They are lazy, sneaky, and violent. Watch out. These Moslems who are taking bread out of French mouths will soon be stealing French girls." Where, young Algerians would like to know, did such notions come from? What's so wrong with being an Algerian?

What is so wrong from the French point of view is that France lost a war to the Algerians. Using largely guerrilla tactics, the Algerians rebelled against French rule. When French President Charles de Gaulle saw that the dragged-out war was costing billions of dollars and thousands of lives, yet there was little hope of victory, he wisely offered the independence the Algerians were fighting for.

Military and political leaders whipped up public sentiment against giving in. They almost stirred up a revolt against de Gaulle. French pride had been hurt.

To later generations this history will matter not one whit. But for the time being it is a principal reason for French prejudice against Algerians. Those who harbor that prejudice don't like the idea of a people who defeated them seeking to enjoy the superior living standards of those they defeated.

The Beribiche children had nothing to do with the Algerian

war. The oldest, Youssef, was only three years old when it finished. Farida was two. The others weren't even born yet. But, like other young Algerians, they have been caught in its wake.

Yet by no means is life all uphill. They get twice as many holidays as their French comrades, because they celebrate the Moslem as well as the great French ones, like July 14th and of course Christmas. Their Christmas doesn't include Christian customs, but what's most important to children is all there: presents, a Christmas tree, and a Christmas feast, generally with lamb as the main course. Algerian parents are human despite their strictness. They couldn't stand the disappointment in their children's eyes if Père Noël visited their school friends and skipped them.

Another high point is mother's cooking. She spends hours in the kitchen combining inexpensive materials into luxurious dishes, of which there is always plenty for everyone. Couscous is an example. It's a highly seasoned mixture of coarsely ground wheat, delicately steamed and re-steamed with butter, bits of meat, and many different vegetables. To prepare a proper couscous requires hours of work and a great deal of patience. The result is rich, mellow, and very filling. The family laps it up by the bowlful in appreciative silence.

The Beribiche children also love the pastries their mother prepares. They especially like the sweet ones, often stuffed with apples. Sometimes they are stuffed with ground meat or fish and served as a main course. The pastry dough is simple—flour, water, and salt. If the pastry is for dessert, sugar is added to the dough, and more sugar is sprinkled on top during the baking. No matter how many of these Mrs. Beribiche makes, they disappear rapidly.

Fruit is always on the dining table, especially bananas, figs, and dates. France imports shiploads of bananas and dates from Africa. Figs grow abundantly in Provence and Corsica. So there's no problem when Mrs. Beribiche puts these fruits on the market list for her sons to fetch. She won't send her girls to shop. That's risking too much contact with males.

The figs and dates the children eat for breakfast. They wash them down with gulps of buttermilk so thickly clotted that it's almost like cottage cheese. Then they are off to school. The trip is short, but in the minds of the children it's a great leap from Algeria to France, from the land of their parents to the land of their playmates, the land they also want to be allowed to claim as their own.

THE CHILDREN of the French island of Corsica have just the opposite view. They are fiercely proud of being Corsican. When they think at all about the mainland country of which they are citizens, they are critical. They criticize mainland laws that apply to all French citizens but are out of keeping with their island style of life. They resent the ugly condominiums that mainlanders have built in Corsica for vacation or retirement homes. They fear that the natural beauty of their island will be spoiled by these big blocks of concrete and glass. "We oughtn't to be part of France," some of them declare. "We ought to rule ourselves."

These are views they hear frequently at home. Corsican families are extra-close; children adopt their parents' sentiments as their own. To understand the desire for independence, one need only consider the Corsican history of being owned by a succession of rulers. Since some three thousand years before the birth of Christ, Corsica has been owned or occupied by Greeks, Romans, European tribesmen, an Emperor of Constantinople, Italians, Arab pirates, Spanish, English, and finally the French.

The French name for the island, Corse, stems from its occupation by Arab pirates: corsair is another word for pirate.

By 1768, when France bought Corsica from the Italian city of Genoa, which owned it, a Corsican independence movement had been well organized by a leader named Pascal Paoli. He is still so revered that his portrait hangs in a place of honor in many Corsican homes.

In the midst of Paoli's revolt, the English sailed in, with the excuse of aiding him, but with the actual intention of taking over the island. Young Napoleon Bonaparte, later to be emperor of France, led Corsicans in an anti-English, pro-French uprising. He and his followers were booted off the island, but in 1796 Napoleon reclaimed his birthplace for France.

The island has been French ever since, but the independence movement that flowered under Paoli is very much alive today. Corsicans express their desire in terms that reflect their particular needs as an island. "Why," say teachers, "must our students go to France for a university education? Why can't we have a university here?" When the teacher of twelve-year-old Christine Attaccioli discusses with her the course of study she must follow to prepare for a French university, Christine says flatly, "I don't want to go to France. I want to picnic in my own mountains and swim in my own sea." Like most Corsican young people, she is a nature-lover.

Actually, a university is planned for Corsica, but the French government proposes to build it in a spot that will require very round-about travel to reach. "You see the trouble?" grumbles one school principal. "Somebody in Paris puts his finger on the map of Corsica and says this looks like a good central place. What he doesn't realize is how many mountains would have to be circled on difficult roads to reach it. Unless, that is, the government wants to build a whole new set of mountain passes."

Out of Corsica's past grows not only the desire for independence, but also the popular language of the people. Christine is taught pure French in school, but she may also take courses in Corsican if she chooses. The language echoes every group that landed on Corsican soil except the English, who remained there only two years. It's a harmony of Italian and French, with overtones of Arabic, Greek, Latin, and Spanish.

Lyrics of the folksongs every child knows are always written in this language. There's one for every occasion. Paghiella for high church services, Lamenti for men going to war, Voceri to work up the spirit of revenge. There are love songs and lullabies, work songs and songs that mock political leaders. Some make fun and some make tears. The tempo is usually waltz or polka. The polka is as accented as the hoofbeats of galloping horses. Always there is a guitar accompaniment that suits the mood of the song. It can be as staccato as castanets, as tinkling as shattering crystal, or as fluttery as a sigh.

The songs have a plaintive quality, even the funny ones. Youngsters often sing about a bandy-legged little fat man chasing a prize sheep that has got loose from the fold. The sheep flees up a mountain, frisking higher and higher, while the man pants after it. The singers imitate his breathlessness. He never does catch up with his sheep. "Which of us," the song asks at the end, "ever achieves his heart's desire?"

Christine goes to the Collège Saint-Paul in Ajaccio, the island capital. She lives in a modern house in a suburb of the city and rides her bike to school. Some of the boys ride *motos*, motorbikes, to the collège. The school yard is full of parked bikes and motos.

The young people are very enthusiastic about their school. From classroom windows they have full views of the sapphire Mediterranean, which, this far out at sea, has lost the pollution that muddies it near the coast of France. Hardly ever, though, do the students look out while classes are in session. They concentrate on their work. When their teacher asks a question, they are all apt to answer at once. They study with a passion. It's prompted by family love. They want their marks to give pleasure at home.

"Please, please," the teacher has to beg. "Raise your hands. Let's talk one at a time."

Reaching school is easy for the students at Saint Paul's, though the bike and moto riders do have to maneuver through some pretty heavy traffic. Transportation takes a much bigger bite out of the day of mountain students. Schools are few and far apart. The first youngster may climb on the school bus as early as six in the morning. In the winter, the bus driver turns on his headlights long before he reaches the last home.

But mountain youngsters are used to that. They believe there's no life quite like theirs, surrounded as they are with all sorts of nature's treats, from chestnuts to cherries.

Eleven-year-old Jacques Colonna lives in the mountain village of La Porta. His home is tall—four stories high—and narrow. The windows are tall and narrow too. The house is built of schist, gray scales of rock from the mountains, and on the outside is as forbidding as a fortress.

Inside it's warm and hospitable, with a spacious kitchen paved with slabs of rock and a high, heavily beamed ceiling. The kitchen table and the benches on either side are carved from the wood of chestnut trees, which abound on the island. A battery of shining pots and pans hangs over the chestnut-wood sideboard.

Jacques's father makes a living from his vineyard, his pigs, and his sheep. He sells most of the meat of the pigs and the milk of the sheep to mainland France. The sheep's milk is used in the manufacture of roquefort cheese and the pigs' meat for hams and sausages. Mainlanders consider Corsican ham a prime delicacy. Jacques often helps milk the sheep. He also helps harvest grapes.

His friends and his three sisters join him in the harvest. They make a game of the work, racing each other to see who can finish stripping a row of vines first. At noon they pause for a picnic. They lunch on *prosciutto*, which Jacques calls in Corsican *prisutti*, razor-thin slices of smoked raw ham. They roll the slices around ripe figs, which they have gathered from nearby trees. Next comes cheese—a blue cheese made from sheep's milk and an extra-strong cheese from the milk of goats. Bread, of course.

A month or so after the grape harvest, Jacques and his friends go chestnut gathering in La Châtaignerie. This is a vast forest of chestnut trees not far from his village. He calls the chestnut tree *l'arbre à pain*, the bread tree, because his mother dries the nuts and makes flour from them. She dries them in a portable fireplace, called in Corsican *fucone*. It's a great square box in which a fire can be laid, which can be moved to any convenient spot.

Corsican chestnuts are much larger than ordinary chestnuts; some grow as big as eight to ten inches around. The trees that bear them are giants too, as tall as sixty feet, with trunks up to twenty-one feet in circumference. Chestnuts are eaten in all sorts of ways—roasted, sliced and fried, or boiled with fennel, or put in soups, pastries, wafer-thin pancakes called crêpes, candies, or stews. Jacques eats some as he picks them. After using a rock to split open the prickle-stiff outer shell, he bites into the raw nut inside. It's very hard. He's lucky he doesn't break his teeth.

What the children don't take, the pigs do, shell and all. Jacques's father herds them into the forest to eat any nuts left lying on the ground. The richness will help make them fat for slaughter.

Along with the nuts, Jacques brings home some of the broad leaves of the chestnut tree. His mother uses them to make baskets, weaving the leaves together with twigs. In the spring Jacques will fill these with strawberries and cherries.

Every other fall he and his father travel a long distance to the *fête de la Santa* in the village of Casamaccioli. The trip is too long to take every year. Jacques and Monsieur Colonna have to start before dawn. They leave Mother and the girls at home. Though women are welcome to attend the ceremony, traditionally it is a man's festival. The two Colonnas wear their best clothes, including their flat-crowned, round-brimmed black hats. On the morning of September 8th, a wooden statue of the Virgin Mary is carried from the village church to a field where, in the afternoon, a fair will be opened. The high point of the festival is the men's singing tournament. The singers, two by two, make up chants in dialogue, composing as they go along. The fair and the tournaments will continue for two more days but Monsieur Colonna doesn't dare leave his animals that long.

Jacques's life in La Porta is very different from Christine's in Ajaccio, where everything is very modern, except perhaps the battered, flat-bottomed fishing boats that crowd the harbor. On holidays they may be arched with palm branches. In among them, crane-crowned freighters and sedate passenger vessels from the mainland give the scene the quality of a double exposure. Which is the true Corsica?

The answer is, both. Christine very much likes to go up to Jacques's mountains to picnic and camp, but to live like a villager? Oh, no. Jacques doesn't even care to come down to her city at all. He's happy where he is. Yet the two have something in common: an intense love of their island, intense pride in being Corsican.

CORSICANS AND ALGERIANS aren't the only people who spice the life-style of the French. For example, meet the gypsies.

Gypsies are believed to have come from northwest India sometime in the first thousand years after the birth of Christ. Romany, their language, is a little like the way people in that region still speak. Today some five million gypsies wander and camp all over the world. They dress in bright clothes, the men with bandanas around their heads, the women in flaring skirts with sequined shawls twinkling over their blouses.

Every year at the end of May, and again at the end of October, gypsies from all Western Europe weekend in a small seaside village in France, Saintes-Maries-de-la-Mer. At these gatherings, it's easy to pick out French gypsies from the others. French gypsies are settled gypsies. They live and work and go to school like other French families. Their language is French. Their clothing is French. Only in summer and on pleasant weekends do they go a-gypsying.

Thirteen-year-old François Moreno, his grandmother, mother and father, five brothers, three sisters, aunt and uncle, and assorted cousins and in-laws live near each other in Montpellier. They attend one of the two festivals annually. François is in his second year at collège. An older brother, Émile, has graduated from collège and is earning some money driving a taxi for the time being. When he has made enough, he plans to enter a lycée d'enseignement professionel, or LEP, and learn to be an auto mechanic.

Émile is vexed with the fixed idea that he finds too many people have of gypsies. "We don't tell fortunes, we don't beg, and we don't steal, the way they seem to think we do," he complains. "We have very strict family morals. If any one of us ever got in trouble with the police, he would be in worse trouble at home.

"Some of our older people do speak Romany still," he continues. "My grandmother does. She is unhappy that I can't speak a word of it and don't care to. Down here," he waves an arm in the direction of the gypsy-jammed streets, "I use sign language to talk to gypsies from other countries.

"Another thing"—he is off and going now with his complaints—"some towns put up signs on the outskirts reading, 'No migrants allowed!' That means us. We're no more migrants than any other family on vacation. We're tourists, just like them. We need to buy food, just like them. Yet if we park in town to buy it, the police are apt to give us a hard time. They don't seem to realize that we are bringing business to the place. I agree there are a few of us who are *voyoux* (rascals). Aren't there in any group?

"One thing people say about us is true," he admits. "We are clannish. We stick together in families. All the relatives stick together. No one is supposed to marry a non-gypsy. It does happen, though. My brother married one. Since *he* couldn't leave the family, his wife joined *us*. The only way a gypsy leaves his family is by dying.

"Come," he adds, "meet my sister."

His sister, Rose, is dancing a *farandole*. This old Provençal dance is performed to a rapid waltz tune, which manages to have the beat of a tango despite its 3/4 time. Various dancers come forward to perform. The others form a circle around the soloist, clapping hands to the rhythm of the music and the dancer's tapping feet. Émile accompanies his sister on his guitar. Snapping her fingers to imitate castanets, she sways and swivels in the center of the circle. A boy moves in to join her. They dance without touching, sometimes face to face, sometimes back to back.

Before this merrymaking started, the gypsies attended a church service in honor of the Virgin Mary, the New Testament figures of Mary Magdalen, Martha, and Lazarus, and a mythical black saint named Sara, whom the gypsies have adopted as their patron saint. Sara was supposedly the servant of the Virgin and Mary Magdalen.

The legend goes that in 40 A.D. these women, with Lazarus,

landed on the spot where the village now stands, having sailed as missionaries from the Holy Land. The festival celebrates their landing.

After church, the gypsies sing, dance, and visit from *campeur* to campeur. A campeur is a home on wheels. More compact than a trailer, it has living quarters, driver's cab, and engine all in one piece. Like many French, gypsies rent them for summertime and weekend travel.

The campeurs are lined up along the low seawall at the edge of the beach. Washing, strung from one to another, flaps in the sea breeze. On the beach itself, children frolic around the orange and blue tents that have been pitched for their night's sleep. At suppertime, the wind carries the smell of charcoal and wood fires and the aroma of good soup.

Tables and chairs are set up under beach umbrellas. Everything is orderly; even the pots and pans are stacked in neat rows on the sea wall. Litter is disposed of in big plastic bags the gypsies have brought with them. After supper, the merrymaking will recommence and continue until the small hours of the morning. The grownups catch thirty winks in the campeurs, but the children in the tents whisper and giggle until sunrise.

On Sunday night, when François, Émile, and Rose return with their family and relatives to Montpellier, children and grownups will all sleep soundly. Monday morning, in school or at work, they will probably still be a little weary from the get-together. There will be a good many gypsy yawns.

THE MORENO GRANDMOTHER, who is sad that her grandchildren don't and won't speak her language, is not alone in her regrets. In Auvergne, Brittany, Provence, the Alps, and the Vosges, most young people no longer speak the dialects of their grand-parents.

But one old language not likely to wither away is that

French With Spice 93

spoken by the Basques in the western Pyrenees Mountains. The families who rode the little train up the mountain called La Rhune in search of Spanish hams and wine are among them. They call their language Euskara. Euskara doesn't belong to any of the world's languages. Scholars who study such matters think maybe Arabic, maybe Hindu, maybe Chinese, or maybe all three somehow influenced the way Basques talk. But nobody really knows. Euskara is a mystery language.

Basques on the other side of the Pyrenees in Spain speak it as well as those in France. The French Basques live in an area that reaches from the city of Bayonne southward to the mountains and eastward to the town of Tardets, a space slightly more than half the size of the American state of Rhode Island. That cubbyhole of France encloses a separate world.

In the eleventh century the ancestors of the people who now live there fished far and wide for whales. After the French settled eastern Canada, the waters off that coast became their favorite fishing grounds. When the English conquered French Canada, the Basques became pirates. They were so feared and so famous that they were permitted to keep their caps on in the presence of the French king, something even the highest nobles were not allowed to do. They were rough-and-tumble characters, these seagoing Basques, and the Basque fishermen of today, who prowl the seas in search of tuna, have kept the dark, tough, wiry appearance of their ancestors.

So have the Basque farmers, who mainly raise sheep, cattle feed, and apples. Like all Basques, the farmers wear their berets at rakish angles. So seldom do they remove them, one might almost think the berets were glued to their heads. But no. They do come off in church.

Espadrilles, the rope-soled sandals of Basque men, have become a fashion in all Europe and the United States. For the

Basque, they are a practical necessity. A hard worker, he's on his feet from dawn to dusk. The rope soles put spring in his step.

Women and girls dress in a lively fashion, and their skirts are attention-getters. Usually they are handmade from rough linen, dyed in brilliant colors and banded at the hem with stripes of contrasting color. The colors and patterns carry over onto the tablecloths and placemats they take to town to sell on market days. Mothers teach their daughters the secrets of turning out these distinctive wares.

Mother and all the children look up to Etcheko Jaun, the head of the family; father, of course. He decides which of them will inherit his house, his herds, his goods. The heir may not be the oldest and is not necessarily a son. Etcheko Jaun chooses the one he considers most fit, regardless of age or sex.

In recent years a number of young Basques who were not chosen have emigrated to the United States or South America to make a living. When they think they have made enough money for their needs, they go home. They are called, in Euskara, Americanoaks.

Some farm families live in villages perched on ledges partway up mountains, some in deep ravines that lead into the spine of the mountains. These many ravines ending in the spine make a map of the Pyrenees look like a fish skeleton.

Fall is the busiest time in this region. Young Basques help gather apples in the orchards that climb the slopes. It's a scramble to harvest fruit from such heights. The clouds, which always linger in the Pyrenees, seem very close.

Fall is fern-picking time too. The ravines are lined with giant wild ferns, called bracken. Their color is the clock for picking time. When they turn brown, young people turn out to help gather them. The thick fronds are often taller than the youngsters, but they manage to wrestle the cuttings onto their orgas, the high-wheeled farm carts drawn by oxen. There may be an argument over who gets to drive the carts home. Etcheko Jaun settles it. The losers pile in on top of the ferns.

At home the carts are unloaded and their contents spread on the barn floor as winter litter for sheep and cattle. In spring the litter, well manured, will be used for fertilizer.

A hard day's work deserves a fine evening meal. Fall is when wild pigeons migrate over the Pyrenees on their way south. If father has trapped some of these in recent days, there will be roast pigeon for supper. To trap pigeons, he and his sons and neighbors and their sons string nets from treetop to treetop. They know exactly when and where to string their nets, because the birds migrate at the same time and follow the same track through the Basque country every year. After the nets are strung, the men and boys climb nearby trees. When they see the pigeons coming, they shout and wave white cloths. The frightened birds dive low in their flight and are caught in the nets.

Another dish that the whole family relishes is *garbure*. This is soup, but too thick to eat with a spoon. It's spread on bread instead. Garbure is made mainly of cabbage and bacon, or other salt meat, along with seasonal vegetables. Mother cooks the mixture in her *toupi*, a huge pot that she keeps well anointed with garlic. She makes *tourin*, onion and tomato soup, and stews stuffed with fowl in this same pot.

Her crockery pot is reserved for *cassoulet*. Her finest cassoulets are made with goose, though she may use other meats when the geese in the farmyard haven't yet been fattened enough to kill. She adds sausage, sometimes salt pork. She drowns the meat in *flageolets*, baby lima beans no bigger than the nail on a child's little finger. She bakes the cassoulet for many hours in a gently warm oven. A light film forms on top during the baking. Seven times she breaks up the film and stirs it deep into the pot. Her mother taught her she must do this. She is teaching her daughters to do the same thing. Whether or not she had goose meat for the cassoulet, she had goose fat. A Basque cook is lost without her supply of goose fat.

Feeding the family's geese during the month when the birds are being fattened for the table isn't much fun. No child can manage the job alone. Two are needed. One holds the goose. The other uses a funnel to pour kernels of cattle corn into its gullet. If the goose won't swallow, the child gently pushes the kernels down with a stick, carefully blunted and polished so as not to injure the bird. The idea is to plump him well for roasting, cassoulets, and other delicious dishes, as well as to make sure of that vital supply of cooking fat.

Lamb is hardly ever on the family table. The wool and milk of Etcheko Jaun's herd command excellent prices. Eating lamb would be like eating money. During summer the sheep are taken to graze in communal pastures. The communal pasture is an old Basque custom. Village representatives get together and buy pastureland. They keep the pasturage in prime condition, with plenty of good nibbling for vast quantities of sheep. The individual sheep herder pays for the privilege of letting his sheep graze on this land. It's cheaper for him to pay rent for fields that others care for than to care for fields of his own. So both he and the pasture landlords profit.

Some of his sheep are milked for making cheese, and all are sheared for wool. Coarse wool is sold for mattress stuffing. Delicate wool, from white ewes known as Basquaises, goes into weaving cloth for fine clothing.

Family homes in the Basque country have a style all their own. Some are roofed in the orange tile of the Midi, especially along the Atlantic coast. Inland they are more likely to be shingled in broad, shaved slices of granite from the mountains. The four corners curl slightly upward, like the corners of a Chinese pagoda. The walls are granite too.

Along the coast, the walls are plaster, often whitewashed. In either case, over the front doorway, the Etcheko Jaun who built the house engraved his name and the date of the building. Later generations have added outdoor balconies with handcarved wooden railings to coastal houses. Basque fathers and sons are fine craftsmen with wood. They enjoy whittling and shaping it into forms of their own designing. They like to carve the mottled wood of myrtle, which grows abundantly in their ravines.

Inside the house is more of their handiwork. Almost every home has a *zuzulu* in the hall, the kitchen, or the dining room, and in the bedrooms as well. A zuzulu is a combination bench, chair, chest, and table. The chest doubles as a bench. The bench has a collapsible back. When upright, the back turns the bench into a chair. When folded to a horizontal position, it extends the bench into a table. Zuzulus come in all sizes, from midget to tremendous.

In the chest section, the family stores all kinds of belongings from toys to tools. Lift the heavy cover of a big zuzulu—and one might even find *palas* and *chisteras*.

The pala is a wooden bat, the chistera a wicker scoop. Bat and scoop are equipment for *pelota*. Pelota is to the Basques what boule is to Provençaux, the game of games. A player, or *pelotaris*, bats a rubber ball, wrapped in wool and covered with hide, against a high wall. Sometimes, instead of using the bat, he flings the ball against the wall with the chistera, a long, curved wicker scoop. When the ball bounces back, it must land within limits marked on a court. The player must send it against the wall again, after no more than one bounce. Like boule, pelota is a game for men and boys.

Practically every village has a pelota court. Frequent tournaments are held among villages. They cause great excitement, with fans rooting for their teams and sometimes bawling out the *chacharia*, scorekeeper and umpire. He's not always as impartial as umpires are supposed to be. He can make sarcastic remarks when a player flubs. His pithy comments amuse fans of the player's opponents and they shout approval. Fans on the player's side try to shout him down.

Like pelota, a number of the folk dances that Basques take part in or watch are performed by men only. In one, the *sauts basques*, Basque leaps, the men hold their bodies still and stiff from the waist up, while they spring high in the air, nimbly moving their feet in ever changing patterns. In another, the dancers whirl around a glass of wine. At the end, each stands for a split second on the glass, without breaking it or spilling a drop. How they manage it is their secret.

The dancers are accompanied by tunes known only to Basque musicians. Their instruments are the *tchirulä*, a three-holed flute, and the *ttun-ttun*, which is a cross between a tambourine and a banjo. Sometimes a fiddle or accordion is added.

As in Corsica, singing comes naturally in the Basque country. The songs describe everyday happenings and are often made up on the spur of the moment. Children may sing about the ferns they are gathering, the apples they are picking, the goose they are stuffing. A tuna fisherman sings a song of rejoicing for a good catch, a farmer for a good sale. On holidays, singers hold contests. Judges assign a theme and a melody. The contestants make up rhymes to express the theme and fit the music.

Also like Corsicans, the Basques are outdoor people. Even the cold of winter doesn't keep children indoors. Stilled by ice, the many streams and rivers formed by waterfalls from the mountains make fine skating alleys. The slopes provide good ski runs.

Winter, summer, fall, or spring, every Sunday is church day. The Basques are deeply devout Roman Catholics. From the small-

French With Spice   9 9

est child to the oldest grandparent, not to attend church on Sunday is unthinkable. More than a few also attend during the week. Once inside the church, the family separates by sex. Boys and men sit in the galleries, looking down on the lace-draped heads of the womenfolk. Their daughters and wives wear *mantillas* to church. They borrowed the style from the Spanish Basques across the border. A mantilla is an ample triangle of lace. The Basque mantilla is handmade, with scalloped edges. It falls in graceful folds, sometimes halfway down the back.

THOUGH THE BASQUE COUNTRY IS, for the most part, a separate world the rest of the modern world hasn't entirely passed it by. Vacation villas thrive along the Atlantic coast; the city of Bayonne is a busy port. In this respect it is like all France, which is a mix of different and alike, of past and of present. Into this four-toned picture French children fit as they grow up.

The genes of history are in the ways they speak, the songs they sing and the holidays they keep. Behind the scenes, history prompts the way they think. Even the sea salt in the food they eat is as much the product of history as of the sea.

But at the same time, a gentle wind of change is refreshing their classrooms. Their government offers the means for low-cost recreation and travel to regions other than their own. It enlarges the output of farmers, and up-to-date transportation brings the good things that result to family tables far and wide.

Not that the young people stop chewing or singing to dawdle over why the food is so savory and the song so haunting. More likely they ask: May I have some more? or What shall we sing next?

Above and above right: The Beribiche children discuss their life in France.

Right: A class at the Collège Saint Paul in Ajaccio, Corsica.

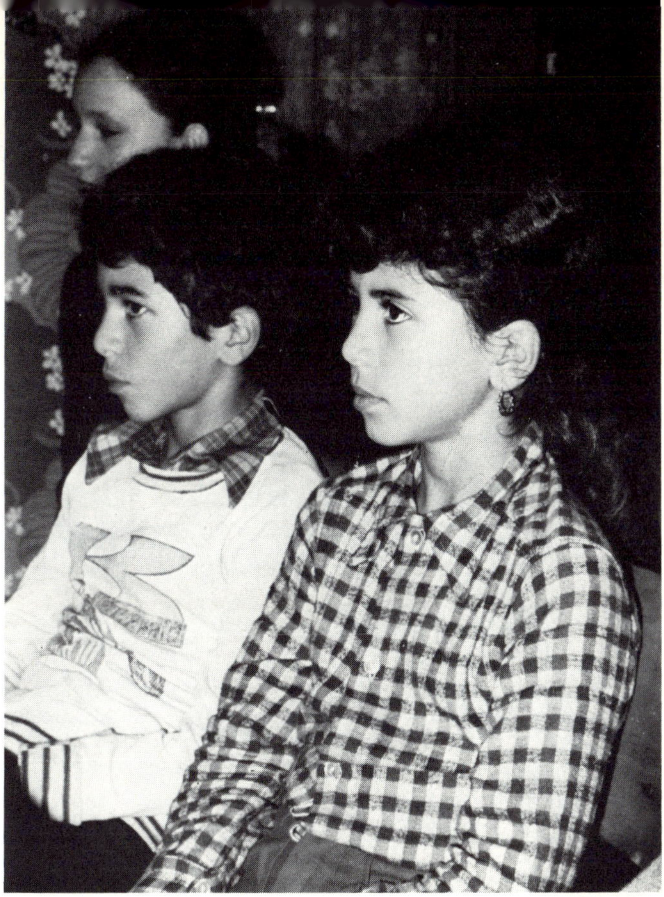

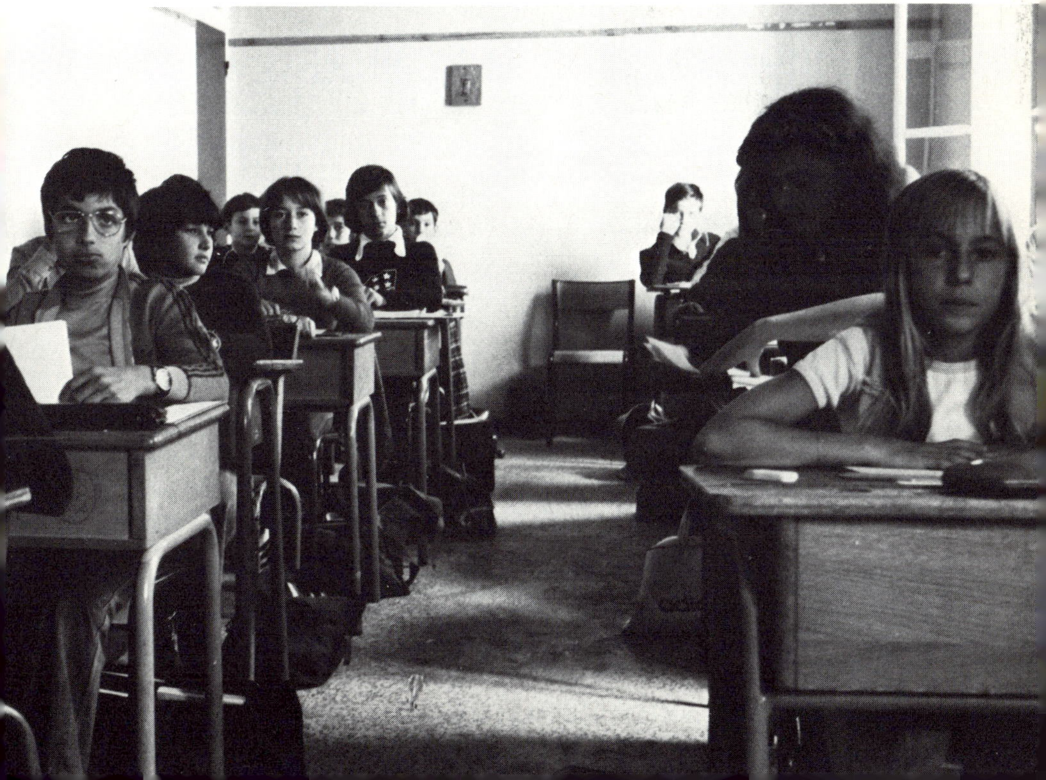

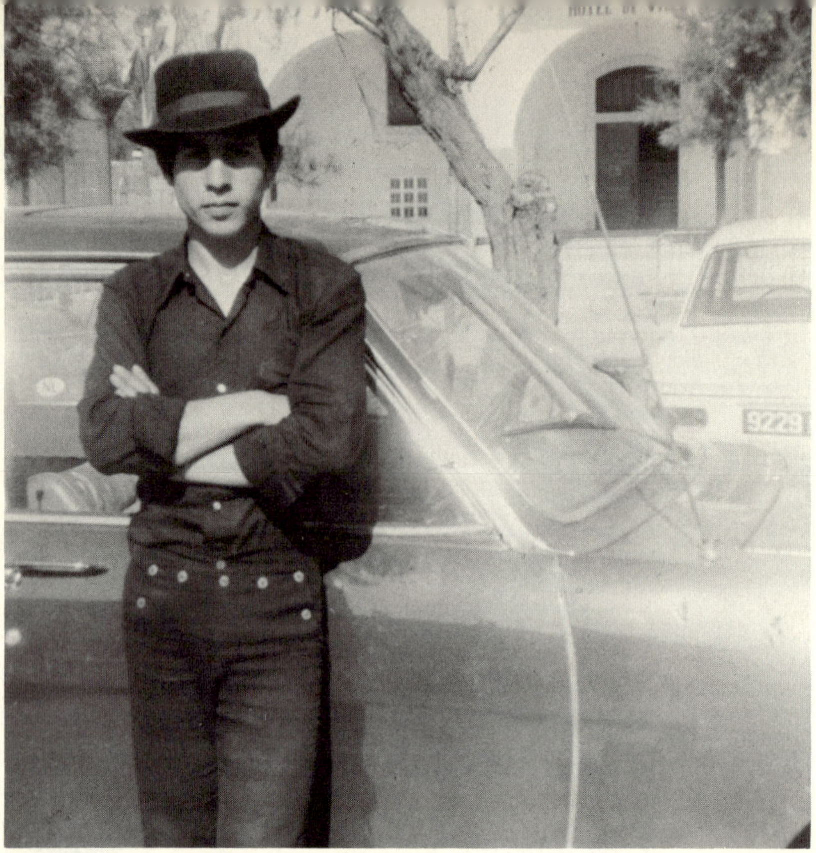
9229

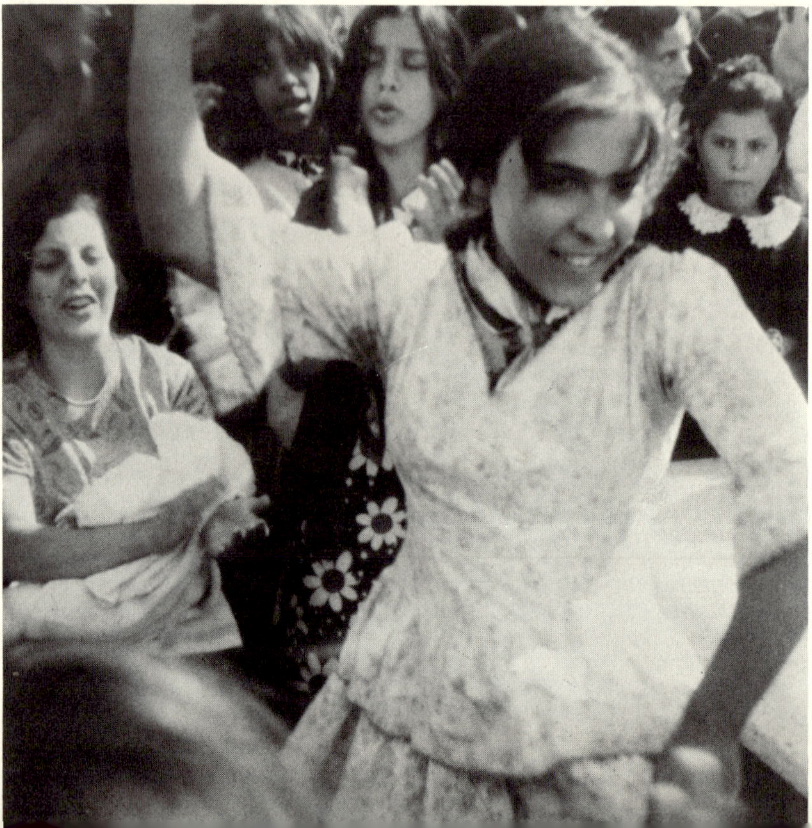

Above left: Emile Moreno drives a taxi to earn money to attend school. AUTHOR'S PHOTO

Below left: Rose Moreno dances a farandole. AUTHOR'S PHOTO

Above: Basque men perform one of their strenuous folk dances. FRENCH GOVERNMENT TOURIST OFFICE

A pelota court in Biarritz in the Basque region. FRENCH GOVERNMENT TOURIST OFFICE

BIBLIOGRAPHY

The acknowledgments listed in the front of this book are really the bibliography, since it is based on field research rather than library research. However, certain reference materials were consulted, as follows:

Chaber, Abdeltrader, *La Jeunesse Algérienne en France*, Société National d'Édition et de Diffusion, Algiers, 1977.

Dandelot, Marc, and Froment-Meurice, François, *France*, La Documentation Française, Paris, 1975.

Dossiers Pédagogiques de la Radio et de la Télévision Scolaires, Centre National de Documentation Pédagogique, Paris, 1977–1978.

Hergé, *Les Aventures de TinTin*, Casterman, Paris, 1949–1978.

Jeunesse et Sports, Dossier Statistique, Secrétariat d'État à la Jeunesse et aux Sports, Division des Études, Paris, 1978.

LaMorisse, *La Ballon Rouge*, L'École des Loisirs, Paris, 1976.

Marchette, Pascal, *Santu du Corse* and *Santu di Corsica*, Flammarion, 1976.

Mathieu, Suzanne, and Veillon, Dominique, *La Famille Française*, La Documentation Française, 1978.

Maurois, André, *A History of France*, Funk and Wagnall's—Farrar, Straus & Giroux, New York, 1968.

Lyon, Raymond; Malezieux, Raymond; Mangin, Stanislas; De Margerie, Philippe; Martinet, Paul; Maunac, Claude; May, Louis-Philippe;

Milleron, Jean-Claude; Moreau, Mlle. Edmée; Norrant, Louis-Georges; Paoli, Louis; Petit, Jean; Raphaël, Petit; Picon, Gaëtan; Picot, Mme. Yvette; Poindroin, Paul; Robin, Dr. Pierre; Leguy, Jean; Senard, Jacques; Stasi, Bernard; Schwartz, Bertrand; Thery, Jacques; Thery, Jean-François; Thibaud, Philippe; Toiron, Jean; Touchard, Pierre-Aimé; Vacquer, Guillaume, *Panorama de la France*, La Documentation Française, Paris, 1969.

Onisep Publications: *Après le Baccalauréat, Après la Classe de Cinquième, Après la Classe de Troisième, Les Orientations Après la Classe de Seconde, Après la Collège d'Enseignement Technique,* Ministère de L'Education, Paris, Année Scolaire, 1976–1977.

Téléformation, Programmes, 1977–1978, Centre National de Documentation Pédagogique, Paris.

For Further Reading

Children who are studying French will enjoy the following books. All of them tell interest-holding stories, and all of them explore some aspect of the lives of their contemporaries in France. Age level has been suggested on the basis of the story. However, a student's facility with the language also needs consideration. Some older students may find the books for younger ones easier to understand.

Le Ballon Rouge, see bibliography. See text for description. Illustrated in black and white. Now available in paperback. Ages 9–11.

Cayrol, Jean, and Mitsumasa, Anno, *Les Quatre Saisons*, Hachette, Paris, Nouvelle edition, 1978. A French village seen as seasons change. Illustrated in color. Ages 8–10.

Cullum, A., and Galeron, H., *Moka, Mollie et Moi*, Harlin Quist, Paris, 1977. Story of a child reacting against adult pressure in school. Color and black and white illustrations, some comic, some poignant. Ages 8-10.

Bibliography

Greg, *Achille Talon et le Trésor de Virgule*, Collection "Achille Talon," Dargaud, Paris, 1977. A bound comic book. Exciting adventure, well written. Ages 10–12.

Le Livre d'Or de la Chanson Enfantine, Les Editions Ouvrières, Paris, 1976. A large collection of French folk songs, old and new. All ages.

Meynier, Yvonne, *Un Lycée Pas Comme Autres*, G. P. Rouge et Or, Collection "Souveraine," Paris, 1978. Life in a French lycée through the eyes of two girls. Ages 12–14.

Pierjean, Anne, *Loïse en Sabots*, G. P. Rouge et Or, Paris, 1977. A story of teenage love, marriage, and death in the Alps during World War I. Ages 13–15.

Saint-Gil, Philippe et Janine, *Le Prince Noir*, G. P. Rouge et Or, Collection "Souveraine," Paris, 1977. The very human adventures of a boy and his black cat. Ages 10–12.

Santu de Corse, see bibliography. The life of a mountain boy in Corsica. With information on language and vegetation. Illustrated in color. Ages 9–11.

Série Contes et Legendes: *Contes d'Auvergne, de Bretagne, de Provence, de Bourgogne, de Normandie*, Hachette, Paris, 1978. Folk tales from various French regions. Illustrated in color. Ages 9–11.

Index

Ajaccio, 86, 89
Animals (farm), 11, 21–22, 30–31, 58–59, 87, 88, 93
Animals (wild), 13
Atlantic Ocean, 22, 27, 28, 73, 99
Attaccioli, Christine, 85, 89
Auvergne, 29, 35

Basques, 93–99
Bayonne, 93, 99
Belledent, Eric, 30–31, 34, 43, 46, 61, 73, 74, 75
Beribiche children, 76–84
Bicycling, 4, 20, 75, 87
Birds, 13, 23, 94
Bonnaud grandchildren, 59, 60, 69, 73
Bordeaux, 27
Brittany, 28, 29, 53, 73
Burgundy, 10, 34

Camping, 16–19, 73, 89, 92
Canada, 93
Chavaniac, 30, 34
Chores, 23–31
Chrétien, Jean, 43
Climate, 4, 12, 24, 51, 64

Clothes, 12, 17, 32–33, 67–68, 79, 90, 93–94, 95–96, 99
Colonna, Jacques, 87–89
Comic books, 38, 51–52, 79
Corsica, 84–89
Customs, 5, 6, 8, 15, 55

de Champeaux, Antoine, 10, 11, 12, 13, 15, 34, 41, 46, 59, 60, 75
de Champeaux, Augustin, 12–13, 15
de Champeaux, Dominique, 10–13, 15, 34, 42, 46, 59, 60, 75
de Gaulle, Charles, 82

English Channel, 28
Excursions, 16–23

Family life, 7, 13–14, 24–31, 59–60, 76–84, 90–91, 94
Farming, 3, 4, 11, 26–27, 64, 93–94, 95
Fishing, 12, 20, 21, 22, 25–29, 93
Food, 5, 6, 7, 12, 20–21, 26, 30, 31, 35, 47, 55–56, 61, 67, 73, 75, 83–84, 87–88

Index

Forests, 11, 13
Frank, Anne, 16–17

Games, 11, 22–23, 64, 97–98
Germany, 41
Government aid to children and families, 4, 10, 30, 35, 41, 45, 46, 57, 59, 73, 99
Guet, Laetitia, 3–10, 12, 19, 34, 40, 41, 42, 46, 52, 61, 69, 73, 75
Gypsies, 89–92

Haby, René, and his school law, 43, 44
Hiking, 15, 16, 75
Holidays: Bastille Day, 71–72, Carnival, 65, Christmas, 59–63, General, 59–75, 80, 83, New Years Day, 63, Pentecost, 65–66, Regional, 66–68, 74, 89, 91–92, 98, Saint John's Day, 71, Three Kings Day, 63
Homes, 6, 10, 30, 86, 87, 96–97
Hunting, 12, 95

India, 89
Italy, 41
Izard, Christopher, 49–50

Language, 3, 15, 32, 34, 36–37, 38, 55, 61, 79, 85–86, 87, 89, 90, 92–93
Louis XIV, 19, 57

Mediterranean Sea, 3, 40, 73, 86
Moreno, Émile, 90–91, 92
Moreno, François, 90, 92
Moreno, Rose, 91, 92
Mountains, 3, 15, 16, 21, 24, 29, 35, 57–59, 62, 64, 74, 85, 87, 89, 93

Movies, 8, 50–51
Musical instruments (played by children), 8, 16

Napoleon, 16, 85

Oyster growing, 27–28

Paoli, Pascal, 85
Parents, 3, 5–7, 9, 11, 13, 15, 20, 24, 77, 78–80, 84
Paris, 12, 22, 23, 71, 76, 77, 85
Parks, 22, 23
Pascal, Rose, 18, 63
Pets, 3, 4, 5, 9, 10, 30, 31, 35, 46, 74, 75
Picnics, 20–21, 56, 85, 87–88, 99
Portugal, 74
Products, 4, 11, 27–28, 30, 87, 93, 96
Provence, 3, 4, 17, 60, 61, 63, 64, 76

Reading, 45, 51–53
Recreation, 4, 8, 9, 10, 16–23, 58
Religion, 59, 68–71, 78, 80, 98–99
Rivers, 3, 4, 8, 9, 10, 11, 22, 27, 53, 98

Saintes-Maries-de-la-Mer, 90–92
Schools: Atmosphere, 34, 35, 36, 39–40, 41, 44–45. City, 36. Classrooms, 33–34, 44–45. Country, 34, 35, 43–44. Exams, 41–42, 43–44. General, 20, 32–47, 77, 78, 86. Methods, 36, 38, 42–43, 45, 53, 81. Subjects, 36–39. Teachers, 34, 38, 44, 45, 85. Trips, 53–58, 64.
Scouts, boy and girl, 16–19, 46, 62
Shopping, 5–6, 25–26

Singing, 13–14, 15, 16, 17, 54–55, 58, 61, 67, 72, 86, 89, 92, 98
Skiing, 57–59, 98
Soulié, Jean-Claude, 44–45, 53
Soviet Union, 17
Spain, 21, 74, 93, 99
Sports, 10, 12, 13, 23, 41, 57–59, 98
Strasbourg, 16, 19, 62
Swimming, 4, 9, 21, 73, 77, 85
Switzerland, 41

Television, 8, 11, 12, 31, 36, 45–46, 47, 48–50

Traffic, 20, 33

United States (Children's concepts of), 8

Vacations, 17, 72–74
Versailles, 57
Vineyards, 4, 11, 26–27, 74, 87

Weekends, 3–23

Robinson Township Library
Robinson, Illinois 62454